Beyoncé and Beyond

This book examines three years of Beyoncé's career as a pop mega star using critical race, feminist and performance studies methodologies.

The book explores how the careful choreography of Beyoncé's image, voice and public persona, coupled with her intelligent use of audio and visual mediums, makes her one of the most influential entertainers of the 21st century. Keleta-Mae proposes that 2013 to 2016 was a pivotal period in Beyoncé's career and looks at three artistic projects that she created during that time: her self-titled debut visual album *Beyoncé*, her video and live performance of "Formation," and her second visual album *Lemonade*. By examining the progression of Beyoncé's career during this period, and the impact it had culturally and socially, the author demonstrates how Beyoncé brought 21st century feminism into the mainstream through layered explorations of female blackness.

Ideal for scholars and students of performance in the social and political spheres, and of course fans of Beyoncé herself, this book examines the mega superstar's transition into a creator of art that engages with Black culture and Black life with increased thoughtfulness.

Naila Keleta-Mae is Principal Investigator of the Black and Free research-creation project, Tier 2 Canada Research Chair in Race, Gender and Performance and an Associate Professor at the University of Waterloo. She has research, teaching and artistic expertise in race, gender and Black expressive culture, and has written and commented on Beyoncé for media outlets including Noisey, CBC and the BBC.

Routledge Advances in Theatre & Performance Studies

This series is our home for cutting-edge, upper-level scholarly studies and edited collections. Considering theatre and performance alongside topics such as religion, politics, gender, race, ecology, and the avant-garde, titles are characterized by dynamic interventions into established subjects and innovative studies on emerging topics.

Rechoreographing Learning
Dance As a Way to Bridge the Mind-Body Divide in Education
Sandra Cerny Minton

Politics as Public Art
The Aesthetics of Political Organizing and Social Movements
Martin Zebracki and Zane McNeill

Lessons for Today from Shakespeare's Classroom
The Learning Benefits of Drama and Rhetoric in Schools
Robin Lithgow

Notelets of Filth
An *Emilia* Companion Reader
Laura Kressly, Aida Patient, and Kimberly A. Williams

Transcultural Theater
Günther Heeg

Shakespeare and Cultural Appropriation
Vanessa I. Corredera, L. Monique Pittman, and Geoffrey Way

For more information about this series, please visit: www.routledge.com/Routledge-Advances-in-Theatre--Performance-Studies/book-series/RATPS

Beyoncé and Beyond
2013–2016

Naila Keleta-Mae

LONDON AND NEW YORK

First published 2023
by Routledge
4 Park Square, Milton Park, Abingdon, Oxon OX14 4RN

and by Routledge
605 Third Avenue, New York, NY 10158

Routledge is an imprint of the Taylor & Francis Group, an informa business

© 2023 Naila Keleta-Mae

The right of Naila Keleta-Mae to be identified as author of this work has been asserted in accordance with sections 77 and 78 of the Copyright, Designs and Patents Act 1988.

All rights reserved. No part of this book may be reprinted or reproduced or utilised in any form or by any electronic, mechanical, or other means, now known or hereafter invented, including photocopying and recording, or in any information storage or retrieval system, without permission in writing from the publishers.

Trademark notice: Product or corporate names may be trademarks or registered trademarks, and are used only for identification and explanation without intent to infringe.

British Library Cataloguing-in-Publication Data
A catalogue record for this book is available from the British Library

ISBN: 978-0-367-40683-7 (hbk)
ISBN: 978-1-032-49195-0 (pbk)
ISBN: 978-0-367-80848-8 (ebk)

DOI: 10.4324/9780367808488

Typeset in Bembo
by Newgen Publishing UK

Contents

Acknowledgements vi

1 Teaching *Beyoncé* 1

2 Self-Titled, 2013 7

3 Formation, 2016 20

4 Lemonade, 2016 29

5 Longevity 40

Index 42

Acknowledgements

Thank you to the undergraduate students who have taken Gender and Performance at the University of Waterloo since I began teaching it with a focus on Beyoncé in September 2015 – your questions and perspectives inform my own. Thank you to the University of Waterloo and Social Sciences and Humanities Research Council for funding aspects of this research. Thank you to Editor Laura Hussey and to Beyhan Farhadi and Keira Mayo for editorial assistance.

1 Teaching *Beyoncé*

I first began to think of Beyoncé as a research subject in December 2013 while watching each of the 17 videos from her self-titled album *Beyoncé*. It oozed so much sensuality. Close-up after close-up showed how toned, thin and hard Beyoncé's postpartum body was. At the time, my daughter was a toddler and my son an infant. My body had not bounced back from either pregnancy and I resented the social pressure I felt that it should bounce back after two pregnancies. Even though I was on the road to loving my postpartum body, when I watched the videos of *Beyoncé*, I felt deeply self-conscious of the softness around my midsection, arms and legs.

I was on maternity leave, breast-feeding, taking care of children and writing. I was trying to figure out what being a mother of two young Black children in my thirties meant. And there was Beyoncé on screen, performing the sensual Le Crazy Horse's Upside Down act in the video "Partition," sauntering down a hallway with a camera recording a close-up of her cellulite and stretch-mark-free posterior in "Rocket," and on a beach in a floor-length translucent maxi dress with a bikini underneath in "Drunk in Love." The whole thing was spectacular. I was inspired. I was also envious. You should have heard me in conversations with other women: "If I had tons of money, trainers, nutritionists, chefs and nannies my body would be toned, hard and soft in the right places too."

Not only did I envy Beyoncé's body and wealth, but I was also envious of her extraordinary professional success. I could not look away. Certainly, the imagery from her self-titled album was arresting and her performances of herself were riveting. But there was something else there too; it was her performance of Black female perfection as a career woman, wife and mother that captivated me. It was its visual perfection that dislodged my insecurities and floated them to the surface. Beyoncé's performance was brilliant and arresting in part because it displayed just the right amount of imperfection to make the perfection seem almost attainable. The more I watched, researched, studied and contemplated the visual album *Beyoncé*, the more I understood

DOI: 10.4324/9780367808488-1

that my initial study of Beyoncé touched nerves in my own insecurities and triggered anxieties that previously had not been as pronounced. Curious, I wanted to better understand how it related to my own experiences of female blackness and Black motherhood and so I decided to research further.

When I joined the University of Waterloo in 2011 as a tenure-track Assistant Professor, the Theatre and Performance program was in the midst of overhauling its program objectives, curricular objectives and course offerings. One of the new second-year undergraduate courses that emerged from the process is called "Gender and Performance" and it was created and offered, in part, because of my research areas of expertise. Our new curriculum was slated to roll out in fall 2015 and it included the inaugural offering of "Gender and Performance." I was familiar with Kevin Allred's "Politicizing Beyoncé" that he began teaching as a special topics course at Rutgers University in 2010. I told my colleagues about my research on Beyoncé's self-titled album and proposed that I use the album's lyrics and visuals as the artistic object of study and they were immediately supportive.

In spring 2015 I was asked, by the Theatre and Performance program, to provide an image and brief write-up about the course for the department's blog that was subsequently revised by the University of Waterloo's communications team. The following text ran below a black and white close-up of Beyoncé from the "Drunk in Love" video.

> Want to study Beyoncé this fall? We don't blame you. The Department of Drama and Speech Communication is offering a course focused entirely on the mega superstar, entitled Gender and Performance (DRAMA 282).
>
> Perhaps it is the mutability of her voice, the impenetrability of her image, the careful choreography of her public persona and the astute manipulation of audio, visual and audio-video mediums that position Beyoncé as one of the most influential performers of the 21st century. Eponymously titled, the "Beyoncé" album is a vexing articulation of contemporary mainstream feminism that has captivated audiences worldwide.
>
> The course will be offered in Fall 2015 to all students and has no prerequisites. Students will analyze videos from Beyoncé's most recent album, use feminist and critical race theories to reflect on the artist's work and create their own artistic responses.
>
> Instructor Professor Naila Keleta-Mae says that "whether or not feminist scholars, activists or artists agree with Beyoncé's discourse, her influence on popular culture is undeniable. I would argue that it would be negligent for those of us interested in gender studies to dismiss the album 'Beyoncé' or its principal artist."

Don't let the course name fool you; this class is all about Beyoncé. "I'm over being a pop star. I don't wanna be a hot girl. I wanna be iconic." – Beyoncé.

("Drama 282")

I thought the course's focus on one of Beyoncé's albums might generate some buzz. I contacted the media and communications people at the University of Waterloo. They too thought it might get some buzz, but they were undecided about whether to promote it prior to the course or after. Unbeknownst to us, while we were going back and forth in our email exchange about the best strategic next steps, the website *That Grape Juice* found the blog on the university's website and wrote a short article that it pushed out to its network, and that was the beginning of a media storm that went far beyond any coverage I could have imagined. Numerous stories were published and broadcasted in multiple languages. I did dozens of print, radio and television interviews that led to citations in publications including *The Canadian Press*, *The National Post* and the *Canadian Association of University Teachers' Bulletin*. I did television and radio interviews for local and national broadcasters including the *Business News Network*, *CTV*, *CJAD* and *CBC*'s "The National" and "Fresh Air." In the years that followed, I had repeat appearances as a panel member on the Pop Culture Panel on *CBC Radio*'s program "q," which had one million listeners across North America at the time. I wrote op-eds on blackness in North America that were published in the *Globe and Mail* and *Noisey*. In each of these media outlets, I was able to talk about gender, performance, blackness and more to demographics and numbers of audiences far beyond what I could ever hope to reach in years of teaching in classrooms.

The media coverage of my "Gender and Performance" course featuring the album *Beyoncé* led to passionate conversations about the role of universities in North American society. There were those who were ecstatic that popular culture in general, and female blackness in particular, would be analyzed with academic rigour – a reminder that the academic tradition of marginalizing women and people of colour is passé. Others were convinced that the inclusion of Beyoncé in a university course signaled the demise of post-secondary education – an irrational fear that obfuscates the obvious: the intellectual rigour of a course is not solely determined by its object of study but also by the instructor's inclusion of materials that are theoretically and methodologically rich. My course, "Gender and Performance," identified the themes of race, feminism and sexuality in one of Beyoncé's albums and then analyzed those themes using feminist theory, critical race theory and performance studies methodologies. In particular, we analyzed key videos in Beyoncé's discography through the themes of feminism, race and sexuality so that students learned to use Black feminist studies, Black studies and performance studies to unpack the lyrics' narratives and the videos' imagery. I learned two invaluable lessons while managing the at times overwhelming media attention and scrutiny that came with announcing my course. The first is to never read the comment sections of any online article or video about your research or teaching. I liken reading the comments to asking students to complete instructor evaluations right after writing a difficult final exam. Nothing good can come out of that. There is very little that is measured, thoughtful or reflective when people respond immediately after engaging with perspectives that challenge them. The other, far more valuable, lesson was that media engagement is an incredibly impactful mode of teaching.

In this book, I will discuss three key artistic moments in Beyoncé's public presence from 2013 to 2016 and, for each of these compelling artistic moments I will consider two larger questions: what did Beyoncé contribute to popular culture through this art? And how does this art resonate beyond popular culture? Chapter 2, "Self-Titled, 2013" contemplates the first significant artistic moment, which is the release of the album *Beyoncé* (also referred to as *Self-Titled*). The album *Beyoncé* is the artist's fifth studio album and at the time of its release was the only one to not have an image of her as the album's central cover art. *Beyoncé* was a record-breaking, internet-crashing, surprise visual album that the artist announced on Instagram on December 13, 2013. In this chapter, I do a close reading and analysis of the video "★★★Flawless" from the visual album because it was in this song and video that Beyoncé featured her alignment with the word feminist. It was the combination of the release of *Beyoncé* and my interest in the lyrics and visuals of "★★★Flawless" that started me on the path of researching and writing the academic journal article "A Beyoncé Feminist" and later to teaching the "Gender and Performance" course that featured *Beyoncé* as its object of study.

Chapter 3, "Formation, 2016" examines the second significant artistic moment, which is the unannounced release of the video and song "Formation" in February 2016 that included Beyoncé's guest appearance in Coldplay's Superbowl 50 halftime performance. Beyoncé clearly and publicly aligns herself with the Black Lives Matter movement in the "Formation" video and when it was released, I accepted an invitation from *VICE* to write an op-ed about it. I wrote my op-ed so that it mirrored what I do in the classroom. It placed the lyrics and visual into larger historical, political and cultural contexts. I mentioned the histories of Black feminism and the Black Panther Party in the United States. I quoted Mae Gwendolyn Brooks, a Black American literary scholar, and talked about Billie Holiday's song "Strange Fruit." My op-ed was one of the most read stories for a day across all *VICE* networks in 24 countries worldwide and the most read story for the week across their 15 music sites worldwide. That research and analysis forms the basis for this chapter.

Chapter 4, "Lemonade, 2016" considers the third key artistic moment in Beyoncé's career, *Lemonade*, her sixth studio album presented as a film released on HBO in the United States in 2016. *Lemonade* marks Beyoncé's further experimentation with the form of the visual album that she had first explored with her self-titled album three years prior. *Lemonade* is a rich portrayal of female blackness that is dense in its visual and lyrical representations of Black masculinity, Black fatherhood, infidelity, financial independence and rage. The chapter traces the performance of these themes through the analysis of some of Beyoncé's older work and contextualizes the themes within a larger body of Black performance traditions, specifically the portrayals of Black girlhood in Black women's theatre. In addition, the chapter briefly examines The Formation World Tour and "Survivor," and concludes with an analysis of Cardi B's "Bodak Yellow."

You will notice throughout the book I talk about myself from time to time. That is just the kind of academic and artist that I am. I have always used my personal experiences and lived experiences as ways of understanding the world. Some call this way of researching and writing autoethnography, some call it autobiography, others call it memoir. I call it my attempt to be Black and free. I call it connected to what Black female artists have long done. We write ourselves into existence through words shared in public and we write ourselves in on our own terms, flawed as they may be. In the case of this book, that means that there will be times when I am not saying anything at all that is directly related to Beyoncé. Feel free to skim over sections that do not resonate with you. No offense will be taken at all.

Works Cited

Beyoncé. "★★★Flawless." *Beyoncé*, Columbia Records and Parkwood Entertainment, 2013.

———. "Formation." *Lemonade*, Parkwood Entertainment, 2016.

——— [@beyonce]. Video announcing new visual album. *Instagram*. December 13, 2013, http://instagram.com/p/h2YFO6Pw1d/?modal=true. Accessed September 1, 2022.

Canadian Association of University Teachers. "Queen B Gets Her Own University Course." *CAUT Bulletin*, September 2015, https://bulletin-archives.caut.ca/bulletin/articles/2015/09/. Accessed October 11, 2022.

Cardi B. "Bodak Yellow." *Invasion of Privacy*, Atlantic Records, 2017.

Csanady, Ashley. "Beyoncé Is Getting Her Own Course at the University of Waterloo. What the Academe Can Learn from Queen Bey." *The National Post*, June 17, 2015.

Delmar, Dan. *CJAD Radio*. June 19, 2015, Montreal.

Destiny's Child. "Survivor." Written by Anthony Dent, Beyoncé and Mathew Knowles. *Survivor*, Sony Music Entertainment, 2001.

"Drama 282 Takes a Closer Look at Music Superstar Beyoncé." *Communication Arts: News Archives*, University of Waterloo, June 3, 2015, https://uwaterloo.ca/communication-arts/news/drama-282-takes-closer-look-music-superstar-beyonce. Accessed September 5, 2022.

"Drunk in Love." *Beyoncé*. Directed by Hype Williams, performances by Beyoncé and Jay-Z. HW Worldwide and Parkwood Entertainment, December 13, 2013.

"★★★Flawless." *Beyoncé*. Directed by Jake Nava, performances by Beyoncé. Columbia Records, 2013.

"Formation." *Lemonade*. Directed by Melina Matsoukas, performances by Beyoncé, Big Freedia and Messy Mya. Prettybird and Parkwood Entertainment, 2016.

Giese, Rachel (host), Naila Keleta-Mae and Monica Heisey. "Kathryn Hahn Talks Transparent, Motherhood and Career After 40." *Uptalk*, season 2, Chatelaine Magazine, September 22, 2016, www.chatelaine.com/podcast/uptalk/episode-2-kathryn-hahn/. Accessed October 11, 2022.

Hunt, Nigel. "Beyoncé Classes at Canadian Universities Tackle Music, Pop Culture, Critical Thinking." *CBC News*, December 26, 2015, www.cbc.ca/news/entertainment/beyonce-classes-university-1.3376647. Accessed October 11, 2022.

Ito, Mary. "Fresh Air." *CBC Radio*, June 19, 2015.

Kanwar, Amber. "What Bay Street Can Learn from Queen Bey." *Business News Network*, August 31, 2015.

Keleta-Mae, Naila. "A Beyoncé Feminist." *Atlantis* vol. 38, no. 1, 2017, pp. 236–46.

La Rose, Lauren. "Beyonce 101: Canadian Researchers Offer University Courses Studying Pop Superstar." *The Canadian Press*, August 28, 2015, www.cbc.ca/news/arts/beyonce-101-canadian-researchers-offer-university-courses-studying-pop-superstar-1.3207221. Accessed October 11, 2022.

Lemonade. Directed by Beyoncé, Kahlil Joseph, Dikayl Rimmasch, Todd Tourso and Jonas Åkerlund, performances by Beyoncé. Parkwood Entertainment, 2016.

"Partition." *Beyoncé*. Directed by Jake Nava, performances by Beyoncé. Columbia Records, 2013.

Pinto, Alexandra. "New University Course 'Focused Entirely' on Beyoncé." *CTV News*, Kitchener, June 23, 2015, http://kitchener.ctvnews.ca/new-university-of-waterloo-course-focused-entirely-on-beyonce-1.2436700. Accessed October 11, 2022.

Pop Culture Panel on 'q'. "Beyonce's Formation is a Powerful 'Statement of Intent'." *CBC Radio*, February 10, 2016, www.cbc.ca/radio/q/schedule-for-wednesday-february-10-2016-1.3441592/beyonc%C3%A9-s-formation-is-a-powerful-statement-of-intent-1.3441600?update. Accessed October 11, 2022.

"Rocket." *Beyoncé*. Directed by Beyoncé, Ed Burke and Bill Kirstein, performances by Beyoncé. Loveless and Parkwood Entertainment, 2013.

"University to Offer 'Beyonce' College Course." *That Grape Juice*, June 10, 2015, https://thatgrapejuice.net/2015/06/university-offer-beyonce-college-course/. Accessed August 29, 2022.

2 Self-Titled, 2013

To some extent it is the mutability of her voice, the impenetrability of her image, the careful choreography of her public persona and the astute manipulation of audio, visual and audio-video mediums that position Beyoncé Giselle Knowles Carter as one of the most influential performers of the 21st century. Her record-breaking self-titled fifth album, released on December 13, 2013, was a vexing performance of 21st century mainstream feminism that captivated audiences worldwide.

The details of the contracts Beyoncé has with corporate stakeholders are private and so there is no way to know the extent to which she controls and manipulates her public image and messages. But what is public knowledge is that she manages herself through her company Parkwood Entertainment, was a writer on each of the 17 songs on the album *Beyoncé* and co-produced all but two of them. As Nava, a director of one of the album's videos, said "[Beyoncé]'s been through this process of taking increasing control over her own career and identity" (Goldberg). In light of the depth of her participation in multiple aspects of the making of her music, it is unlikely that in 2013 she was at a point in her career where she was a corporate puppet who did and said what she was told. Therefore, when Beyoncé explicitly takes up feminism in the visual album *Beyoncé*, it is at the very least in part because she wants to. Now, whether or not feminist scholars, activists or artists agree with the feminist discourse in her album, her influence on popular culture is tremendous and undeniable. As such, this chapter uses feminist theory, critical race theory and a performance studies methodology to explore the origins, possibilities and limitations of Beyoncé's explicit use of feminism in her self-titled album.

Beyoncé describes herself as a "modern-day feminist" (Cubarrubia), and the feminism she calls for and portrays in *Beyoncé* is hypersexual, über rich and politically ambiguous. Beyoncé, the commercial brand, is a compelling mythical display of capitalist female perfection – one that is categorically unattainable for those unable to mobilize entire industries at their behest.

DOI: 10.4324/9780367808488-2

Beyoncé, the celebrity, is what I would describe as a capitalist's feminist; one who often attributes her phenomenal success to the trope of the American Dream – the seductive narrative that the right blend of hard work and determination will lead to anyone's success. The power in and problem with this trope is that there is just enough truth in it to make it possible to forget other very real factors like access to resources, gender presentation and the like that contribute to, and to some extent determine, the parameters of one's success.

Even a cursory comparison between Beyoncé and other Black female pop stars from 2013 to 2016 – such as Rihanna, Cardi B and Nicki Minaj – makes abundantly clear that Beyoncé was the most successful and accomplished woman in the industry at the time. Beyoncé's command of popular culture was exerted not only through her songs, concerts and interviews but perhaps most notably through her production company's astute use of the modes of distribution online that are ubiquitous in 21st century popular culture. When Beyoncé releases audio, visual or audio-video products they are able to seep into the back and foreground of girls, young women and women's lives as well as the minds of those who make up her male fan base. Beyoncé has consistently articulated her awareness of her impact on girls and young women and she has described the ways in which she has found it stifling to fully express herself within the confines of her perceived responsibility to her fans and popular culture.

To some extent Beyoncé exemplifies what Black feminists have long fought for – the right to her own body, a full professional career and resources to significantly influence her individual experiences. And yet, when coupled with the sheer magnitude of her influence, her choice to emphasize her individuality simultaneously differs from what Black feminist work, focused on the collective, has historically sought to do. This point is exemplified in the song lyrics where Beyoncé instructs women to kneel in recognition of her greatness. These lyrics made their controversial debut in the song "Bow Down / I Been On" and reappeared on her self-titled visual album in the song "★★★Flawless."

On March 16, 2013, Beyoncé posted a picture on her social media Tumblr account with a link to a three-minute and 35 second digital audio recording that opens with the lyrics to the song "Bow Down / I Been On." The lyrics are written to strongly suggest an autobiographical component; they command the female listener to acknowledge and respect that Beyoncé has dominated popular culture since their childhood. In addition, she asserts that she remains an ambitious person despite having been married to hip hop mogul Sean "Jay-Z" Carter since 2008 and being largely absent from the public eye after the birth of her daughter Blue Ivy in 2012.

The recording "Bow Down / I Been On" is comprised of two distinct songs: the first minute and 30 seconds is "Bow Down" produced by Hit

Boy, and the final two minutes is "I Been On" produced by Timbaland, Polow Da Don, Sonny Digital, Planet IV and Keyz. When this song was released, some folks were upset. How dare Beyoncé tell women to bow down and call women bitches? It was a bit surprising coming from Beyoncé, who had first been introduced to the mainstream as a founding member of a cute girls' group called Destiny's Child. But was it really that audacious for her to suggest that she was living the life that she and so many girls dreamed of living? Was it really that far-fetched for Beyoncé, then an inarguably accomplished and leading pop star, to say that her competition should accept that she has defeated them?

I was certainly thrown when I first heard the lyrics. It seemed like a stark departure from her public persona. It was certainly the antithesis of what has become Michelle Obama's oft-recited directive that "when they go low, we go high." But in retrospect, is it that unreasonable for Beyoncé, the most accomplished pop star in the pop star game, to tell women to bow down and call them bitches if she so chooses? Can a Black woman, especially a perennially accomplished one, tell others in her professional circle that they should, in no uncertain terms, admit to and recognize the magnitude of her accomplishments? And while much of the critique, my own included, emphasizes the ways in which Beyoncé's lyrics are misogynist it must also be stated that misogyny and capitalism go hand in hand. In the hierarchical structures that capitalism requires, someone must be at the top and others must aspire to attain their position. Black women all across North America, the Caribbean and, I dare say, much of the world know how to be and play nice – it is a requisite daily act not only for our survival but also for that of our friends, families and communities. Surely there must come a time when we can use all of the expertise at our behest to play hard and state our beliefs clearly, even if it means we are not perceived of as "nice"?

The image Beyoncé posted on her Tumblr to announce "Bow Down / I Been On" was of herself as a child, wearing an elaborate floor-length pink dress replete with lace, overlay and what appears to be crinoline. A small gold crown with red details sits atop her head of coiffed loose brown ringlets. A red pageantry sash is draped over her right shoulder, the words illegible. Beyoncé is framed dead centre; she stands on gleaming hardwood floors in front of a fireplace with an ornate gold screen and a wide white mantel. On the floor behind her sit two large trophies; on either side of her stand at least two larger trophies that tower well above her head and from which other red pageantry sashes are draped and hung. Atop the white mantel are no less than nine golden trophies and one large shimmering tiara. In the midst of all of these displays of competition and success, Beyoncé stands poised, hands placed neatly on either side, lips glossy, smiling comfortably. Superimposed on the image in white full cap typeface are the words "BOW

DOWN." The picture contained a link to Beyoncé's SoundCloud account where a song entitled "Bow Down / I Been On" was available to listen to and share for free. In 2014, less than a year after its release, the song had been played on SoundCloud alone a total of 9,426,226 times and reposted from SoundCloud to other social media sites 40,868 times. These numbers, of course, completely fail to capture the numerous other ways music files are shared across digital media which renders the tracking of the song shares virtually impossible.

The lyrics of this song left the internet divided; the explicit use of the word "bitch" was a departure from Beyoncé's catalogue that includes the song "Run the World (Girls)" – a pop culture manifesto of female empowerment that constrains female agency to heterosexual displays of sexuality. "Run the World (Girls)" features a protagonist, Beyoncé, who tells "the boys" that they fail to possess the veracity of character necessary to hold court with her and she bolsters "her girls" with lyrics that harken to the transnational power of female-identified people to lead the world. The chorus of the song is the repetition of a call and response with each answer declaring females as at the forefront of leadership initiatives and actions worldwide in all sectors. The problem with these lyrics, from my vantage point, is that the insistence on calling women girls infantilizes women and feeds into larger social norms (namely misogyny and capitalism) that often result in the oppression of Black people. When stripped of the captivating production qualities of the music and video, the song's lyrics tell the familiar tale of female agency residing in women's capacity to control men through sexuality.

Beyoncé has long described one of the objectives of her art as the empowerment of young women: "[M]y music is bigger than just performing and dancing and videos. I have a voice and I try to – to teach women how badly we need each other, how much we need to support each other and how anything that you really want, you have to work for" ("Encore") The juxtaposition of Beyoncé's talk of female solidarity with her request in "Bow Down / I Been On" for women to supplicate before her is noteworthy. That said, for those of us whose professional lives are not and will never be fodder for international scrutiny and presumably forever enmeshed in history, we can have contradictory views that few, if any, will ever notice, much less scrutinize. In other words, sometimes I, and I think others who consider Beyoncé's art, forget that she is an artist and a human being. Now, that "forgetting" is not accidental – it is evidence of the narrative of superiority and exceptionalism that popular culture demands from its stars. It is a narrative that Beyoncé brilliantly performs with all the discipline and control of a master performer who has plied her trade for more than 20 years in an entertainment industry that is notoriously fickle and patriarchal.

Beyoncé has long combined her voice and public persona with an astute manipulation of audio and visual media to tell the stories she wants to tell to the audiences she wants to reach. That is a tremendous amount of power for an African-American woman to have harnessed in a country that has anti-Black racism as a core component of its founding. In the case of the Beyoncé song "Bow Down / I Been On," some argued that her use of the word "bitch" in the song was an extension of the braggadocio culture of hip hop. It is important to note that the connotative meaning of the word "bitch" was undergoing a shift in popular culture around 2013 that was arguably led by Black lesbian, gay, bisexual and trans culture in the United States.

Former YouTube sensation turned famed podcaster, stand-up comedian and current scriptwriter Kid Fury and his friend Crissle host a widely popular podcast called *The Read* that provides explicit, comedic coverage of popular culture. Around the release of Beyoncé's self-titled album, Kid Fury and Crissle were hardcore, unapologetic Beyoncé fans who spoke about her ad-nauseam. In a gushing review of one of Beyoncé's concerts, they described how in their euphoria of seeing "Queen Bey" perform, Kid Fury said "I called her so many bitches" and Crissle said that as she stood on her seat screaming "bitch" others looked on upset ("On the Run" 00:37:11; 00:10:40–00:12:10). This led Crissle to clarify in the podcast, "Don't worry about me calling Beyoncé a bitch, it's all out of love. Clearly, I am not calling her like a stank ass, ho ass, trollop ass bitch" (00: 27:09–00:37:02).

The argument about whether language can be reclaimed, if it was harmful to a group of people and be used in new ways, is an ongoing one. Some argue that we can reclaim language; others, including what bell hooks argues of harmful images, disagree and instead think it is a "fantasy" (hooks et al. 00:38:45). As hooks said, "I used to get so tired of people quoting Audre [Lorde]'s 'the master's tools will never dismantle the master's house' but that was exactly what she meant – that you are not going to destroy this imperialist white supremacist capitalist patriarchy by creating your own version of it even if it serves you to make lots and lots of money" (hooks et al. 00:38:55–00:39:17).

Beyoncé says that she recorded about 80 songs for the album *Beyoncé* and selected songs that she says were "more effortless for me, that stuck around, that I still loved just as much as I loved a year ago when I recorded them" ("'Self-Titled': Part 3" 00:23–00:26). She chose to tell women to supplicate to her greatness with the release of "Bow Down / I Been On" in March 2013, and she chose to continue her message in "★★★Flawless," but this time she affixed it to an excerpt from the feminist discourse of Chimamanda Adichie's TEDx Talk "We Should All Be Feminists."

On the evening of December 13, 2013, Beyoncé's Instagram account posted, to its then 30 million followers, a video that appeared as a thumbnail image of a black square with all caps block font in a light pink with hints of grey that spelled out the word "Beyoncé." The caption that accompanied the thumbnail/video was "Surprise!" The video was 30 seconds long and it was comprised of short clips of music videos, excerpts from songs and the words "Beyoncé Visual Album 14 songs 17 videos available now" (@Beyoncé). Her Instagram followers quickly alerted everyone online that the album was available on iTunes and could only be purchased as a complete album – all 14 songs and 17 videos. And who can forget Crissle's memorable reaction to the album's release captured in her Google Live chat with Francesca Leigh Ramsey that night? If you haven't seen it, head to your nearest internet browser and find it – it is that good (Ramsey 00:06–00:34). It gives a visceral sense of the pandemonium and sheer joy that Beyoncé's surprise release brought to her fans.

Within 12 hours, Beyoncé's "Surprise!" caused 1.2 million tweets. Within the first three days it was number one on iTunes in 104 countries (Apple Press Info). Beyoncé's "Surprise!" took the internet by storm. What made the release of *Beyoncé* innovative was that an artist of Beyoncé's stature had never before released a full-length album without any promotional materials whatsoever, not to mention the staggering, unprecedented feat that is the production of 17 music videos, each boasting full production values. It is remarkable that Beyoncé's team managed to keep this project a secret given the number of people involved in recording each song and creating each video, which is further evidence of the discipline and control that Beyoncé has long had over all of her public appearances. Beyoncé describes the impetus behind the surprise album as a combination of her desire to communicate directly with her fans and have her fans experience her album as an entire art project as opposed to giving them the ability to buy singles (" 'Self-Titled': Part 1" 02:16–03:15). I also suspect that it is more profitable to sell entire albums than it is to sell singles.

Beyoncé is an undeniably astute and highly successful capitalist in an entertainment industry in which commercial success is notoriously fickle and fleeting. She says she only competes with herself and that prior to starting a new album she reviews her most recent chart positions and aims to surpass those numbers ("Beyonce on Piers Morgan Tonight" 37:53–38:01). So, when Beyoncé chooses to explicitly address feminism, as she does in the song "★★★Flawless," we can presume at least two things: 1) the song will be heard by millions of people worldwide – especially the girls, young women and women who are her principal demographic and 2) she has deduced that the kind of feminism she chooses to articulate and endorse will be financially lucrative. It is this carefully constructed and executed rubric that permits Beyoncé, in the song "★★★Flawless," to call women bitches who need to bow down in acknowledgement of her stature mere moments before she features the following extended 50-second compilation of excerpts from Chimamanda Ngozi Adichie's "We Should All Be Feminists" TEDx Talk:

> We teach girls to shrink themselves, to make themselves smaller. We say to girls, "You can have ambition, but not too much. You should aim to be successful but, not too successful otherwise you will threaten the man." [...] Because I am female I am expected to aspire to marriage, I am expected to make my life choices always keeping in mind that marriage is the most important. Now marriage can be [...] a source of joy and love and mutual support but, why do we teach girls to aspire to marriage and we don't teach boys the same? [...] We raise girls to see each other as competitors, not for jobs or for accomplishments, which I think can be a good thing, but for the attention of men. We teach girls that they cannot be sexual beings in the way that boys are. [...] "Feminist: the person who believes in the social, political, and economic equality of the sexes." (00:12:15–00:28:06)

Beyoncé said that she happened upon Adichie's lecture when she was watching videos on YouTube about feminism ("'Self-Titled': Part 2" 01:50–02:04). Now, some academics scoff at the notion that someone would go online to try to find out about a complex idea like feminism. But my response to their disdain is to echo what Amber J. Philips and Jazmine Walker have expressed repeatedly on their podcast *The Black Joy Mixtape* and that is that feminism is not solely the domain of academics and the intellectual elite. Feminism – especially Black feminism – is for all women regardless of where or how we get our information. It is reprehensible to shame, mock or dismiss the means by which any woman (including Beyoncé) finds herself in the word feminism or in the politics the word conjures for her.

When listened to in its entirety, Adichie's TEDx Talk is a thoughtful and engaging lecture about the relevance and place of feminism in contemporary Nigeria. Beyoncé's decision to ignore the rich body of Black feminist work from African-American women is an intriguing one – instead she makes a foray into transnational Black feminism, one which simultaneously brought Adichie's voice, name and literary body of work into popular culture in North America. And, based on the notoriety Adichie gained by being included in Beyoncé's song, she went on to have her TEDx Talk published into a book that included a press tour.

The video for "★★★Flawless" opens with a nod to Beyoncé's childhood as an entertainer; the footage of Ed McMahon on *Star Search* introducing the performance of "the hip hop rapping Girls Tyme" followed by a brief shot of the six girls, including a nine-year-old Beyoncé, as they perform the first dance move of their routine – a high kick. The archival footage transitions into black and white footage of the legs of someone in torn fishnet stockings, a plaid skirt and weathered black boots. Other lower limbs are visible in this shot too: one pair in distressed faded blue jeans with black leather boots and a pair of feet in well-scuffed black leather lace-up boots. And then there is a shot of Beyoncé, head bowed, one knee slightly bent, wearing a pair of frayed, torn, acid washed, cut-off jean shorts and a black leather belt with large metal detailing. She is wearing fishnet stockings, high-heeled black leather boots with elaborate chain detailing and a long-sleeve plaid shirt tucked in at the waist – rolled up to just below the elbows and buttoned all the way up to the top. Her hair is a wavy, asymmetric blond bob with dark roots, lowlights and highlights.

The cement ground of the interior shot is littered with bits of debris and the wall behind Beyoncé, which appears to be cement, is visibly cracked with various layers of paint at varying stages of peeling. Just above her head is the word "flawless" in a dark all caps font that was put onto the wall in a purposefully uneven way so that the letters are incomplete but clear enough to be legible. The shadows cast in this establishing shot loom large in this dank, filthy, derelict building as the slowed-down footage emphasizes Beyoncé rolling her head and pretending to punch herself in the cheek. Cut to two shots of tall thin white men, one styled in ways that reference a skinhead, the other reads as a punk rocker and then it is back to Beyoncé; this time with her back turned to the camera and her hands against the wall in a shot that shows the back of her costume. The cut-off jean shorts deconstruct into a jean thong with fishnet fabric that forms hemlines. The video is populated by men and women dressed and coiffed like skinheads, punks and rude boys who dance, kiss, lounge, push and mosh on a filthy cement floor and abandoned leather furniture. The atmosphere is hard, aggressive, sexual; the surfaces are cement, leather, graffiti; the people are white, brown, Black and tattooed and they move in a cinematography that suggests that violence and sex lurk just below the surface. The set, camera work, performances and production values culminate to create an artistic and compelling video with aesthetics that are the antithesis of the song's title – "flawless".

Beyoncé turns and faces the camera just in time to mouth the opening verse about other women dreaming as children for an adulthood like Beyoncé's reality. She tells them to never forget that their dreams are her reality and concludes that they should venerate her. But Beyoncé's lips cease to move and her eyes harden into a cocky glare when the word "bitches" plays. I read Beyoncé's performance of not mouthing the word "bitches" as both a nod to and disavowal of all of the critiques about her use of the word in "Bow Down / I Been On." Her refusal to mouth the word in her audio-visual performance permits her to conveniently sit on the fence in a controversy that she caused when she first called women "bitches" in "Bow

Down / I Been On." When taken out of its original context and affixed to the tail-end of Beyoncé's call to be worshipped, Adichie's words become an endorsement of sorts; a container meant to justify Beyoncé's braggadocios and misogynist lyrics.

Beyoncé has a history of responding to criticism in this kind of measured, strategic and indirect way. She sang the US national anthem at President Barack Obama's second inauguration and a mild controversy erupted in the media when it was revealed that she had lip-synched the words to the song. Several days later at a press conference to discuss her upcoming performance at the NFL Superbowl 50 Halftime she entered the room, asked the press gallery to stand and gave an excellent acapella performance of the national anthem – an indirect response to the criticism she had received. Similarly, when an audio-less surveillance video of her sister Solange physically attacking Beyoncé's husband in an elevator was released in 2015, it trended on social media and in the tabloids. Days later, Beyoncé's team issued an innocuous press release that was followed, several weeks later, by a surprise release on Beyoncé's website of a remix of "★★★Flawless" done with rapper Nicki Minaj. In the remix, Beyoncé attributes the mêlée in the elevator to the realities of living a life of extraordinary wealth – specifically her and her husband's then combined net worth of one billion dollars. All this to say that Beyoncé does not just drop or ignore the moments when her name is in the news for reasons she deems unfavourable or unflattering; instead, she often crafts some kind of indirect response which is, I would argue, precisely why feminism, and a textbook definition of it, were centred in Beyoncé's pop culture sphere. And in those moments, the cultural phenomenon that is Beyoncé fused misogyny and feminist rhetoric in popular and financially lucrative ways.

It is contradictory and complex. Sometimes listening to "★★★Flawless" reminds me of reading Joan Didion's book *The Year of Magical Thinking* in which she documents the year after her husband's death. In the book, Didion mentions knowing, as she was living through the mourning, that she would write about it, which means that she knew that she would artistically explore her pain in ways that would further her career and what, precisely, is wrong with that? I enjoyed Didion's book and recall no general consternation or public debate about what it meant for her to profit from pain. Beyoncé said that when she wrote the lyrics about bowing down that appear in "★★★Flawless," she had reached a point of frustration and that those were the words that came out. The song lyrics are written from the perspective of a female protagonist who, like a champion prize fighter, is assertive, confident and competitive. She cleverly uses words to constantly assert her dominance to potential contenders, excite her fan base and frustrate her detractors and that is precisely what the original iteration, "Bow Down / I Been On," did upon its release. The decision to release the song and not add it to Beyoncé's catalogue of unreleased material is one that reflects the lyrics in the song "Grown Woman" from the same album in which Beyoncé declares her autonomy to choose which factors to prioritize in her decision-making.

In 2014, Beyoncé was featured on the cover of *Time Magazine*'s "100 Most Influential People" issue; an event that she describes as "definitely one of the goals in my life. It's something important for me as an artist because it's not about fashion or beauty or music it's about the influence I've had on culture" (qtd in "'Time' Releases"). The magazine cover is not one of the plethora of glamour shots of Beyoncé that populate the internet; nor does the black and white image conjure the familiar tropes of success, sexuality and power that one might expect from a mainstream publication's proclamations of listing the "100 Most Influential People." The cover Image in question features Beyoncé with a despondent facial expression. She is clad in white high-waisted underwear, a white halter bra top and a sheer white crew-neck top with elbow-length sleeves. The sleeve of the left arm is rolled up to her shoulder and the other is down. The hem of the shirt is partly tucked into the upper right-hand side of the underwear. The roots of her hair are dark and lighten into wispy, straight, almost invisible strands that end in a slight curl near her waist. It is an image that drew the ire of bell hooks, who in a live-streamed panel discussion said about it:

> I wish I brought in the *Time Magazine* with Beyoncé on the cover because one could deconstruct for days that first she's looking kinda of like a deer in headlights and she's wearing the little panty and bra set, you know that some of us wore like when we were 10 or 12. And I'm thinking, "Isn't this interesting that she's being supposedly held up as one of the most important people in our nation, in the world. And yet why did they image her, I mean she's not glam on the cover of *Time Magazine*; what is that cover meant to say about the Black female body? (hooks et al. 00:31:28–00:32:04)

In my estimation, hooks' presentation of her reading of the image reflects, at least in part, hooks' attentiveness to the presence of the live audience at the panel and, as such, a desire to captivate them. Nonetheless, hooks raises a fair question about the implications of pairing an infantilized image of Beyoncé with text about her influence in the world. However, even though hooks assumes that Beyoncé was styled for the *Time Magazine* cover by the magazine's employees, I would suggest that given Beyoncé's stature it is more reasonable to assume that she had significant influence over how she was styled. Were the latter true, it would require that her image be read not as explicit coercion by proxies of corporate stakeholders but as Beyoncé's choice. Erin Hatton and Mary Nell Trautner's research on the sexualization of women on *Rolling Stone* magazine covers offers productive insights into what 'choice' means for female entertainers with enough cultural resonance to be featured on a cover. Hatton and Trautner conclude, "whether or not women 'choose' to be sexualized, the sheer repetition of their sexualization *in combination with* the intensity of their sexualization (but not that of men) suggests that there is very little that is 'individual' about such choices. Instead, we argue, it is necessary to identify the social forces that shape and constrain individual choice" (74, emphasis in original).

In Beyoncé's case, three social forces include historical legacy, celebrity culture and corporate expectations. Her historical context is informed by the legacy of Black women who were staged as working sexual objects on auction blocks across the United States during the transatlantic slave trade. Another social force that influences the range of choices Beyoncé has available with regards to her visual representation is her celebrity status as hip hop culture's "southern belle" with a voluptuous body and lyrics rife with sexual agency (Durham 41). From a business standpoint she has been described as "an industry" (Cashmore 142) and it is one she vehemently protects, as evidenced by her statement, "I've worked too hard and sacrificed too much to do something silly that would mess up the brand I've created all of these years" (Beyoncé qtd. in Cashmore 142). It is facile for some to read Beyoncé's choices around her visual representation as those of a vacuous pop star performing a vexingly familiar narrative of female blackness as sexual and non-threatening. But the reading I am suggesting here is that of a businesswoman and performer who successfully performs the notes required by the social forces that delineate the boundaries of her choices while also subverting them.

On the *Time Magazine* cover, that subversion is visible in Beyoncé's gaze that has a hint of an edge to it. In a sense, Beyoncé disrupts her own brand with a performance within her own performance. I am thinking here of Stuart Hall, who argues that cultural identities are "[n]ot an essence but a *positioning*" (395, emphasis in original). Beyoncé uses performances of her self (in visual and audio-visual mediums) to position and re-position herself for the consumption of her audience's boundless fantasies of her gender, sexuality, race, class and age. In other words, not only is she disciplined but she is also incredibly calculating – but then again, which Black person in North America can afford not to be? Some argue that Beyoncé's feminism is vacuous rhetoric wielded to monetize feminism and affix it to the Beyoncé brand. Her introduction of the word feminism to her work in 2013 was an extension of her astutely managed and highly successful career that was at that time built, in large part, by her ability to perch perfectly on the fence when it came to her political views. In the case of the album *Beyoncé* and the song "★★★Flawless," while fence-sitting Beyoncé spins a captivating tale about a woman who is hypersexual, über rich, supremely confident and politically ambiguous – a woman who rehearses and subverts capitalist patriarchy while performing messages of female empowerment.

When Beyoncé pinned her call for women to kneel before her to Adichie's call for gender equality, she attached a chorus that spoke specifically to a flawless physical aesthetic – one that she acquired effortlessly, simply by waking up. This emphasis on looks is a key component of how Beyoncé brands her feminism, which at first glance to some – me included – seemed trite and misplaced. But I now think that it is a huge mistake to fail to recognize that, with one song, Beyoncé gave popular culture an aesthetic representation of feminism and brought feminism into the mainstream. Beyoncé made her Black self the physical manifestation of 21st century feminism and she made feminism palpable, arrogant and powerful when the term had little place in popular culture.

Works Cited

Adichie, Chimamanda Ngozi. "We Should All Be Feminists: Chimamanda Ngozi Adichie at TEDxEuston." *TED Talks*, April 14, 2013, www.ted.com/talks/chimamanda_ngozi_adichie_we_should_all_be_feminists?language=en. Accessed September 4, 2022.

Apple Press Info. "BEYONCÉ Shatters iTunes Store Records with 828,773 Albums Sold in Just Three Days." December 16, 2013, www.apple.com/ca/newsroom/2013/12/16BEYONC-Shatters-iTunes-Store-Records-With-Over-828-773-Albums-Sold-in-Just-Three-Days/. Accessed September 2, 2022.

Beyoncé. "Bow Down / I Been On." *Beyoncé*, produced by Tmbaland, Polow Da Don, Sonny Digital, Planet IV and Keyz, 2013. *SoundCloud*, July 21, 2014, https://soundcloud.com/beyonce/bow-down-i-been-on. Accessed August 29, 2022.

———. "Grown Woman." *Beyoncé*. Parkwood Entertainment, 2013.

———. "Run the World (Girls)." *4*. Parkwood Entertainment, 2011.

———. "Encore: Interview with Beyonce." Interview by Larry King. *Larry King Live*, CNN, April 26, 2009. Transcript, https://transcripts.cnn.com/show/lkl/date/2009-04-26/segment/01. Accessed September 1, 2022.

———. [@Beyonce]. Video announcing new visual album. *Instagram*. December 13, 2013, http://instagram.com/p/h2YFO6Pw1d/?modal=true. Accessed August 29, 2022.

Beyoncé and Nicki Minaj. "Flawless Remix." *Beyoncé: Platinum Edition*. Parkwood Entertainment and Columbia Records, August 2, 2014.

"Beyonce on Piers Morgan Tonight, June 27, 2011 (Full Interview) [HD 720p]." *YouTube*, uploaded by TopQualityBeyonce, June 28, 2011, www.youtube.com/watch?v=KThKNMo8tFM. Accessed September 4, 2022.

Cashmore, Ellis. "Buying Beyoncé." *Celebrity Studies* vol. 1, no. 2, 2010, pp. 135–50.

Cubarrubia, RJ. "Beyonce Calls Herself a 'Modern-Day Feminist.'" *Rolling Stone Magazine*, April 3, 2013, www.rollingstone.com/music/music-news/beyonce-calls-herself-a-modern-day-feminist-250462/. Accessed August 29, 2022.

Didion, Joan. *The Year of Magical Thinking*. Knopf, 2005.

Durham, Aisha. "Check on It: Beyoncé, Southern Booty, and Black Femininities in Music Video." *Feminist Media Studies* vol. 11, no. 1, 2012, pp. 53–60.

"★★★Flawless." *Beyoncé*. Directed by Jake Nava, performances by Beyoncé. Columbia Records, 2013.

Goldberg, Haley. "LAFF 2014: 'Beyoncé' Visual Album Comes to Life at Screening." *Los Angeles Times*, June 14, 2014, www.latimes.com/entertainment/movies/moviesnow/la-et-mn-laff-2014-beyonce-visual-album-comes-to-life-at-screening-20140614-story.html. Accessed August 29, 2022.

Hall, Stuart. "Cultural Identity and Diaspora." *Identity: Community, Culture, Difference*, edited by Patrick Williams and Lauran Chrisman, Routledge, 2013, pp. 392–403.

Hatton, Erin, and Mary Nell Trautner. "Images of Powerful Women in the Age of 'Choice Feminism.'" *Journal of Gender Studies* vol. 22, no. 1, 2013, pp. 65–78.

hooks, bell, et al. "bell hooks – Are You Still a Slave? Liberating the Black Female Body | Eugene Lang College." *YouTube*, uploaded by The New School, May 7, 2022, http://youtu.be/rJk0hNROvzs. Accessed September 2, 2022.

"On the Run." *The Read*, hosted by Kid Fury and Crissle, July 17, 2014. *SoundCloud*, https://soundcloud.com/theread/on-the-run. Accessed August 30, 2022.

Phillips, Amber, and Jazmine Walker. *The Black Joy Mixtape*, 2016–2018.

Ramsey, Francesca Leigh. "Best Stan Reaction to New Beyoncé Album Release ft. @Crissles." *YouTube*, uploaded by chescaleigh, December 15, 2013, https://youtu.be/g1VwnS3OfrY. Accessed September 1, 2022.

"'Self-Titled': Part 1. The Visual Album." *YouTube*, uploaded by Beyoncé, December 13, 2013, http://youtu.be/IcN6Ke2V-rQ. Accessed September 4, 2022.

"'Self-Titled': Part 2. Imperfection." *YouTube*, uploaded by Beyoncé, December 17, 2013, www.youtube.com/watch?v=cIv1z6n3Xxo. Accessed September 4, 2022.

"'Self-Titled': Part 3. Run 'N Gun." *YouTube*, uploaded by Beyoncé, December 25, 2013, www.youtube.com/watch?v=uPmX4ASAcaE. Accessed October 12, 2022.

"'Time' Releases List of Top-100 Influential People in the World." *CNN Breaking News*, CNN, April 24, 2014, www.cnn.com/TRANSCRIPTS/1404/24/cnr.06.html. Accessed September 4, 2022.

3 Formation, 2016

February 6, 2016

It is Saturday evening. I am surfing online. I randomly check my work email. Can I just pause for a moment to talk about how much, at that point in my life, I allowed my job to intrude into my personal life? There I was, checking my work email on a Saturday night. I would like to come clean and say that at the time, checking my email during non-work hours and thinking about work during non-work hours and just working in general during non-work hours was a pretty normal thing for me to do. But to be fair, that was before I got a proper unfiltered taste of how violent and discombobulating professional work environments can be for Black women and women-identified people in Canada. Learning to compartmentalize my work has been a necessary cognitive skill that I have developed to manage being a Black woman academic in Canada. To be more precise, learning to compartmentalize what takes place in formal places of learning in Canada is a skill I have had to develop since elementary school, refine as a graduate student and hone as a tenure-line professor. This is, in part, because academic institutions have long required the conceptual annihilation of blackness and those who do not accept whiteness as the litmus test for normalcy.

That Saturday night, I checked my work email inbox and found an email from a staff writer from *Noisey* (part of the *VICE* network), who sent me a link that he says is to a new Beyoncé video that is unlisted on YouTube. He says the song is called "Formation" and asks if I want to write an op-ed about it. I nonchalantly click the video link and casually watch. I am stunned. Who is this version of Beyoncé? Where did she come from? And frankly, where has she been? I watch the Superbowl 50 halftime performance the next day. The voice of Big Freedia in "Formation" announcing that she, and by extension Beyoncé, is focused and will not be sidetracked by anyone else echoes in the back of my mind. I write late into the night, exceeding the word count I had been given because there is just so much to say. My op-ed is published

DOI: 10.4324/9780367808488-3

the following morning and it is entitled "Get What's Mine: 'Formation' Changes the Way We Listen to Beyonce Forever." In the coming days it is translated into multiple languages and becomes one of the most-read stories across all *Noisey* sites in 15 countries for a week and across all *VICE* networks in 24 countries for a day. That op-ed forms the basis of this chapter with ideas extended through the addition of new material.

Beyoncé's "Formation" is a masterclass in how pop artists can clearly articulate political views that differ from the mainstream without being labelled didactic and marginalized by the media. The video can be read as a manifesto of sorts – a sister-to-sister call to action to dispatch whoever and whatever is in the way. The lyrics tell a singular story of a woman conquering her haters and inviting others to do the same. Beyoncé references the accusations and theories that have floated for years that her and her husband Jay-Z belong to a secret society called the illuminati. For most of the close to five-minute video, Beyoncé's lyrics dress down those who doubt her abilities and at times she rallies other women of her ilk to destroy her doubters with her. Beyoncé concludes with a lyric, sung with an unwavering gaze from below the brim of a low-slung black hat, about how obtaining financial wealth is the most impactful form of vengeance.

The message of economic wealth being the ticket or panacea for all social ills is certainly not a new one to be delivered in the United States of America. What is notable about "Formation," however, is its clear pitch to African-American women – especially in terms of the video's visuals. Sure, me and other Black people around the world have been able to see ourselves in "Formation" too but that is in part because Black people in the United States have long dominated international pop culture. In other words, Black people who are not from the United States are accustomed to decoding African-American culture and finding points of connection with it because we are inundated by it. "Formation" also could not have been quietly relegated to the ether of the internet because it is such a good pop song. Its mainstream trap beat is skillfully created by producer Mike WiLL Made It; the lyrics – co-written with Rae Sremmurd's Swae Lee – provide just the right amount of braggadocio and one-liners; the looks, styled by Shiona Turini and Marni Senofonte, got the attention of bloggers; and the video direction by Melina Matsoukas delivers the right artsy-pop-documentary feel.

The song and video are notably complex meditations on female blackness, the United States of America and capitalism, and the blackness that this song and video articulates is not some kind of abstract, cool, costume that can be put on and taken off at will. This female blackness is specific. It is 26 brown-skinned Black women of multiple shades and shapes dancing in step. It is dark basements and large mirrors where queer Black male hips twerk and revel. It is sun aversion, high-collared dresses, corsets and spread thighs. It is a recording of Messy Mya's voice asking what happened to New Orleans. It is Black women's braless breasts bouncing in hallways lined with bookshelves and brocade. It is homes underwater because in 2005 Hurricane Katrina broadcasted to the world that systemic and institutionalized anti-Black racism were very much state-sanctioned and real. "Formation" is Big Freedia, the queen of bounce music, announcing on behalf of Beyoncé and herself that they are here to dominate not participate. The video of "Formation" is Gucci Spring 2016, Chanel pre-Fall 2016, vintage and custom clothing. It is Beyoncé's declaration that she may very well be the next Bill Gates in terms of wealth and perhaps also in terms of influence.

The video is a breadth of Black cosmologies where worship happens on streets, verandas, floats, churches and parking lots. "Formation" is blue hair, piercing eyes and rows of snatched wigs for sale. It is Black heterosexual marriages where wives are non-monogamous and reward their good lovers with restaurant visits, shopping trips, helicopter rides and career support. It is the words "Stop Shooting Us" spray-painted on a wall in the background. "Formation" is a magical place where police cars sink under the weight of female blackness; where white riot squads surrender to Black boys' rhythmic complexity; and where Black girls play ring games unbothered and uncontained.

"Formation" is a newspaper called *The Truth* with a picture of Martin Luther King Jr. and the words "Why was a revolutionary recast as an acceptable Negro leader?" on the cover. "Formation" is a warning to mainstream media not to attempt to strip Beyoncé of the politics born of her Creole Texas Bama blackness. But it is also a warning to Black people to lay off of the respectability politics that obsessively dissect and admonish Beyoncé for things as absurd as one of her daughter's hairstyles which, for the record, Beyoncé likes styled as an afro.

The impact of "Formation" is derived precisely from this rich multivocality. Mae Gwendolyn Henderson argues that Black women writers have long used multiple voices in their work because it allows them to "communicate in a diversity of discourses." Not as a means to integrate into the white mainstream but instead to "remain on the borders of discourse, speaking from the vantage point of the insider/outsider" (Henderson 264). In the video and Superbowl 50 performance of "Formation," Black women are literally choreographed into lines and borders that permit them to physically be both inside and outside of a multitude of vantage points. And what that choreography reveals is the embodiment of a particular kind of 21st century Black feminist freedom in the US – one that is ambitious, spiritual, decisive, sexual, capitalist, loving and communal.

In the weeks after the "Formation" video was released online and the song was performed at the Superbowl 50 halftime show, some critics were convinced that Beyoncé was simply monetizing Black grassroots community organizing with her performance's references to Black activist traditions – namely the Black Panther Party. Black men randomly recited to me, with a wink and a confident nudge, their paraphrased version of the song's chorus wherein "information" replaces "formation," allowing them to emphasize the need for women to educate ourselves. I could barely keep my eye-rolls contained. Who has long been not only informed but at the heart of Black organizing in North America? Black women. Black women have been holding it down forever. One could argue that Beyoncé simply updated the aesthetic and gave us a cute heeled black lace-up combat boot to consider as a wardrobe option.

In terms of content and presentation, "Formation" is an excellent political pop song and video, but the breadth of its reach and impact is made possible because of Beyoncé's marketing and business acumen. Without any warning, "Formation" came out the day after what would have been Trayvon Martin's 21st birthday and the day before the Superbowl 50 that Beyoncé was scheduled to perform at. Earlier this evening I was at one of my local grocers. A white middle-aged man ahead of me in line bought five bottles of Arizona green tea and a pack of Skittles. I thought instantly of Trayvon and nearly cried. How could people not talk about "Formation" regardless of whether they wanted to engage with its overt endorsement of the tenets of the Black Lives Matter movement? How could folks not speculate about whether Beyoncé would perform it at Superbowl 50 the next day? Beyoncé's unannounced release of "Formation" on the eve of the United States' premiere sporting event turned Coldplay's halftime show into an opening act for the live premiere of her new song about female blackness, race in the United States and capitalism. Her performance was followed by a commercial advertising upcoming ticket sales for her next tour. As discussed in Chapter 2, Beyoncé gave her first masterclass in 21st century music industry marketing and business when she released her self-titled album in December 2013. It was then that she established that she no longer needed traditional marketing to release her music and have it be financially viable. In the months that followed, postings to the same Beyoncé Instagram account that propelled her self-titled album's success slowed while uploads to her personal website increased. I doubt most pop stars would have had the confidence to walk away from actively attempting to grow an audience of more than 30 million people in 2013. Beyoncé did. It seems she decided to invest more into her own website and other platforms. Therefore, it is unsurprising that less than three years later she released "Formation" as an unannounced song to the streaming service Tidal (founded by her husband) and an unlisted video that quickly racked up views on YouTube.

There is an unflinching and relentless quality to Beyoncé's performance of herself in "Formation." She called women bitches and told us to kneel before her in 2013. This time she tells women to fall in line, demonstrate their abilities and be excellent or otherwise they will be dropped. Black American feminists of the 1970s and 80s asserted that women needed to work together in order to survive heterosexism, racism, patriarchy and misogyny. What is fascinating about the lyrics in "Formation" is that the Black feminist capitalism that Beyoncé endorses is not about survival, it is about complete domination – the instruction is to "slay" and, in fact, a woman's ability to "slay" is a key requirement of her involvement. And while this stance certainly has the potential to alienate an array of women, it also can serve as a clarion call to raise the bar in terms of Black women's expectations of what we can make of our lives – even in the face of the very real forms of violence and oppression that we face.

Angela Davis argued that when Billie Holiday put her cover of Abel Meeropol's song "Strange Fruit" (with its visceral description of the lynching of Black people) in the middle of her live set in 1939 she changed the lens through which all of her previous songs should be seen and altered the lens through which any future songs should be heard. "Formation" is that song and video in Beyoncé's career. There is a clarity, cohesiveness and command of aesthetics, lyrics, imagery, politics and pop culture in "Formation" that is profound and immeasurable. Her catalogue should no longer be listened to in the same way.

Beyond its resonance and importance to her own career, "Formation" is perhaps most impactful as a blueprint for other mainstream artists on how to unequivocally delve into the politics that matter to them while simultaneously holding mainstream attention. The Superbowl 50 halftime performance was a visceral reminder of what Black music was and could again be in the United States. In the year that marked the 50th anniversary of the formation of the Black Panther Party, Beyoncé's 28 Black female dancers dominated the stage in signature black berets, heeled combat boots, afros and black leather. It was an ode to the Black civil rights era on the altar that is the Superbowl stage in the United States. Just as Billie Holiday's cover of Meeropol's "Strange Fruit" inspired social awareness, "Formation" had the potential to usher calls for Black freedom from anti-Black racism, state-sanctioned violence and institutionalized poverty to the forefront of Black popular music. And it was impactful, as evidenced by Kendrick Lamar's 2016 Grammy performance of his songs "The Blacker the Berry" and "Alright" later that same year and A Tribe Called Quest's performance of their songs "Award Tour," "Moving Backwards" and "We the People" at the 2017 Grammy Awards. Regardless of how well it is executed, the move to align popular Black music with grassroots organizations' efforts to advocate for rich Black life is a change that would serve Black people well.

The video for "Formation" not only referenced historical movements for Black liberation but also, astutely, gestured towards the Black Lives Matter movement specifically in the scene where the words "Stop Shooting Us" are on a brick wall behind a Black boy as he break dances in front of police officers. It is worth noting as well that the song's lyrics are not equally explicit in their engagement of matters of police brutality or abuses of power by law enforcement officials, and therein lies another example of Beyoncé's expertise as a pop star who creates, observes and reflects popular culture. By keeping the song's lyrics devoid of the most potentially inflammatory subject matter that the song's visuals take up (the alignment with the Black Lives Matter movement) she ensures that her fans, especially the non-Black ones, can sing along to "Formation" without declaring any allegiance to or concerns about Black people or Black culture.

Yet, Beyoncé's performance of "Formation" at Superbowl 50 still drew the ire of many – including police officers – and included some calls to boycott her, which she responded to by creating and selling merchandise soon thereafter that read "Boycott Beyoncé." The impact of the three words "Black Lives Matter" cannot be overstated. This simple statement of fact – innocuous in many ways because it is so obvious and to some extent trite – has nonetheless infuriated some because, I would argue, it cuts right to the heart of a flawed logic of white supremacist belief. As countless others before me have researched, proven and theorized, many dominant, historical and contemporary conceptions of whiteness hinge on the erroneous idea that white people are superior to everyone else – especially to Black people. The words "Black Lives Matter" trouble this logic of racial superiority by succinctly and effectively refusing the conception of Black life as inferior.

In an open letter written in 1984 and published in *Sister Outsider*, Audre Lorde critiqued Mary Daly's book *Gyn/Ecology* because, Lorde argued, it included Black femaleness solely as a site of oppression. In the open letter, Lorde expresses her "grave reluctance" to voice her criticisms, not only because of the complexities of the subject matter but also because of the relationality of those involved. Lorde writes:

> The history of white women who are unable to hear Black women's words, or to maintain dialogue with us, is long and discouraging. But for me to assume that you will not hear me represents not only history, perhaps, but an old pattern of relating, sometimes protective and sometimes dysfunctional, which we, as women shaping our future, are in the process of shattering and passing beyond, I hope.

(62)

Let me write about this pain, this sadness and this disappointment. Lorde let us know that hope is labour, work, unpaid. And hope is required of Black women when we seek to be heard and understood by white women in matters pertaining to female liberation.

I am a Black bisexual woman with decades of professional experience working with white heterosexual and white queer women in social justice efforts in a wide range of public and private organizations and industries. I find it impossible to imagine a North American social reality where justice, including female liberation, is realized without substantive engagement with the theoretical, activist and artistic contributions of trans, queer and cis Black women and Black people in North America. Simply put, if blackness, Black queerness, and Black feminisms are minimized or excluded from white feminist work, then justice, including female liberation, will forever be unattainable.

So, please, let me take a moment here to write about the tightness in the jaw that so many of us, Black queer women, hold from clamping down on our words, thoughts, feelings, life in the face of white femaleness and white feminism. Let me write about the many conversations that I have with Black women, who work in a range of occupations across North America, about how white women in positions of power that exceed our own talk about feminist solidarity while mobilizing their whiteness to rarefy, erase and contain Black women.

Let me write about all that white femaleness requires Black women to ignore because often when Black women share our full unfettered truths it seems to feel like fire to some white women. The violence that white women have directed towards Black women traces its lineage in North America through the era of chattel slavery to the present. One of the vestiges of the persistence of that violence is that Black women pay close attention to white women – especially to white women in positions of power. This occurs in large part because the lives and livelihoods of Black people, Black communities and Black culture have long been entangled with white women's notions of security, benevolence and empathy. White women know it and Black women know it, and it is precisely this knowing that can render solidarity between Black and white women "uneasy" (Roediger).

January 21, 2017

The Women's March was held in protest of the inauguration of Donald Trump as the 45th President of the United States. I stand at the Ontario Legislative Building known as Queen's Park in Toronto with a dear friend and our children. I feel good, self-congratulatory, vaguely righteous. I spot a Women's March button on the ground; I pick it up and glance at the image. There are three facial profiles: one red, one blue, one white. The mouths are open in various states of elocution. I note the angular lines of the noses and the cowlicks of the hair and know that the organizers were not thinking of women or women-identified people who look like me when this button was approved for distribution. My nose is flat and broad. My hair is tightly curled. I pin the button to my lapel anyway, accustomed to these moments of erasure in mainstream feminist movements. I think of writer Arundhati Roy who, when asked about the role of artists in times of war, said, "the role of the artist is not different from the role of any human being: you pick your side and then you fight. In a country like India, I'm not seeing that many radical positions taken by writers or poets or artists, it's all the seduction of the market that has shut them up like a good medieval beheading never could" (Roy 57:39–58:04). I was at the Women's March. I had picked my side. I was fighting. My interest in feeling self-righteous trumped the nagging familiar feeling of omission in grand gestures of female solidarity.

But my righteousness gave way to unsettling questions as I marched with the tens of thousands of other social justice-minded women, men and non-binary people around me. Where had I been for the Black Lives Matter marches and the Missing and Murdered Indigenous Women's marches prior to 2017? Where had I, and the other tens of thousands of people gathered at Queen's Park in Toronto, been? Why do so many of us only show up when the protest is middle class, socially acceptable, predominantly white? A few days later I was listening to the podcast *The Black Joy Mixtape* in which the hosts, Amber J. Philips and Jazmine Walker, discussed a speech given by Erika Hart at the Women's March in Philadelphia. Hart, a Black queer woman, delivered a thoughtful critique of the March's centring of a white feminism that omits non-white women and women-identified people. Hart asks,

> Who is this for? [...] I stand here for those who did not receive marches all over the country when their bodies were under attack, those constantly on the front lines. Have you noticed who is NOT here? I ask that you notice moving forward and get intentional about inclusivity. Start asking in all of the spaces you occupy and take up: Who is this for? And then make it for them.
>
> (4:40–7:11)

Hart's speech raised new questions for me: what does it mean to bring together people to protest after the fact when it is all symbols and little to no actual risk? What are we willing to risk to ensure the health, prosperity and human rights of all women?

Works Cited

"A Tribe Called Quest Performs at the Grammys 2017." *Vimeo*, uploaded by Fatima Robinson, November 26, 2018, https://vimeo.com/302978618. Accessed October 12, 2022.

Beyoncé. "Formation." *Lemonade*, Parkwood Entertainment, 2016.

"Coldplay's FULL Pepsi Super Bowl 50 Halftime Show feat. Beyoncé & Bruno Mars! | NFL." *YouTube,* uploaded by NFL, February 11, 2016, www.youtube.com/watch?v=c9cUytejf1k. Accessed September 5, 2022.

Davis, Angela. *Blues Legacies and Black Feminism: Gertrude "Ma" Rainey, Bessie Smith, and Billie Holiday*. Random House, 1998.

"Formation." *Lemonade*. Directed by Melina Matsoukas, performances by Beyoncé, Big Freedia and Messy Mya. Prettybird, 2016.

Hart, Erika. "Erika Hart @ The Women's March on Philadelphia." *YouTube*, uploaded by Philly Women Rally, January 21, 2017, www.youtube.com/watch?v=PROVSWtIxwg. Accessed September 1, 2022.

Henderson, Mae Gwendolyn. "Speaking in Tongues: Dialogics, Dialectics, and the Black Woman Writer's Literary Tradition," *Colonial Discourse and Postcolonial Theory, A Reader*, edited by Patrick Williams, Routledge, 2013, pp. 257–267.

Keleta-Mae, Naila. "Get What's Mine: 'Formation' Changes the Way We Listen to Beyonce Forever." *Noisey*, VICE, February 8, 2016, www.vice.com/en/article/6e48wm/beyonce-formation-op-ed-super-bowl-performance-2016. Accessed October 12, 2022.

Lamar, Kendrick. "Grammys 2016: Watch Kendrick Lamar's Stunning Performance." *The Verge*, February 15, 2016, www.theverge.com/2016/2/15/11004624/grammys-2016-watch-kendrick-lamar-perform-alright-the-blacker-the-berry. Accessed October 12, 2022.

Lorde, Audre. *Sister Outsider: Essays and Speeches*. Crossing Press, 1984.

Phillips, Amber, and Jazmine Walker. *The Black Joy Mixtape*. 2016–2018.

Roediger, David. "Making Solidarity Uneasy: Cautions on a Keyword from Black Lives Matter to the Past." *American Quarterly* vol. 68, no. 2, 2016, pp. 223–248. https://doi.org/10.1353/aq.2016.0033.

Roy, Arundhati. Interview with Amy Goodman. "Arundhati Roy on India, Iraq, US Empire and Dissent," *Democracy Now*, May 23, 2006, www.democracynow.org/2006/5/23/arundhati_roy_on_india_iraq_u. Accessed September 1, 2022.

4 Lemonade, 2016

April 23, 2016 marked an unprecedented moment in Beyoncé's career. With the release of her sixth solo album, *Lemonade*, we witnessed a female Black mega pop star pivot firmly from pop to politics and still maintain mainstream appeal. Beyoncé's *Lemonade* is a surprisingly complex experimentation with content and form. The film version of *Lemonade* is a nuanced contemplation of the trope of Black masculinity and its devastating impact on Black girls, Black women and Black mothers. The film's main storyline is that of a Black woman and parent in a monogamous marriage with a Black male spouse who has not been monogamous. The extent to which *Lemonade* is an autobiographical account of the marriage of Beyoncé and Jay-Z is unknown. Regardless, *Lemonade* brings into question the Black masculinity that Jay-Z helped popularize and commercialize as a leading figure in hip hop's move from Black culture to mainstream. It is a Black masculinity that is often portrayed as promiscuous, violent and emotionally unavailable and it is a portrayal that is rooted in the same narratives that have been projected on to Black men since the transatlantic slave trade.

At one point in *Lemonade*, Beyoncé holds a séance with her girlfriends in the dilapidated living room of a once grand family home. By the end of the scene the entire house is ablaze in what can be read as a symbolic burning down of the institution of marriage. *Lemonade* is not the story of a Black woman in a bad marriage who stays for the children or who stays because she cannot find another partner or who stays because she does not have the economic means to leave. Quite the opposite, in *Lemonade*, Beyoncé is explicit about her capacity to thrive financially outside of her marriage. In "Don't Hurt Yourself" the female protagonist rejects her lover's money because she has her own and in "Sorry" the protagonist makes clear that she can provide well, not only for herself, but for her offspring too.

In 2003, Beyoncé concluded her debut solo album with a song called "Daddy" in which she sings that she wants a husband who is like her father. It has been widely reported that Beyoncé's father, Mathew Knowles, was

DOI: 10.4324/9780367808488-4

not monogamous while in a monogamous marriage with Beyoncé's mother, Tina Knowles. In *Lemonade* 13 years later, Beyoncé sings the song "Daddy Lessons" about a father who tells his daughter that the man she is pursuing is like him; therefore, the man cannot be trusted, and she should end things immediately. The lyrics are not about a father apologizing to his daughter for the havoc his infidelity has wreaked on their family, nor do they include promises to do anything differently. Instead, the lyrics assert that a woman should never trust men who practice their masculinity the ways that her father does. At the end of *Lemonade*, the protagonist remains in the marriage making the film and album a story from pain to redemption – an unsurprising artistic choice for an album by an artist whose repertoire includes numerous redemptive songs about love.

Nazera Sadique Wright's identification and analysis of age markers as integral to the examination of 19th century literary depictions of Black girlhood informs her assertion that "Black girls needed to find strategies to protect themselves and find a future at an early age. They had to find a way or make one" (10). Sometimes that way was to be assertive and visible, as is the case with the Black girl character Lilacs in Shirley Graham Du Bois's play *I Gotta Home* published in 1942. In other instances, Black girlhood is portrayed as an incoherent state of being, as is the case in Adrienne Kennedy's play *A Rat's Mass* published in 1966. The tropes of Black girlhood born out in the work of 19th century Black writers included among them the "'Loud Girl,'" the "'obedient Christian girl'" and the "'prematurely-knowing girl,'" each of whom had foisted upon them "tremendous responsibility of representing the race in everything they did and said" (Wright 180). In Ntozake Shange's play *Daddy Says*, the two Black girl protagonists are sisters whose mother died at a rodeo while competing on horseback and who are currently being raised by their widowed father. As I have discussed in "Black Girl Thought in the Work of Ntozake Shange," Shange creates a world where Black girls have tough life experiences and draw from Black girl thought to assess their situation and adjust their thinking and their actions. In Beyoncé's catalogue of songs, "Daddy Lessons" is a country music bop. Its raspy vocals are catchy and the story of being taught from a young age to be wary of boys and men is one with personal resonance. It reminds me of one of my great-grandmothers, Beryl West, who told me to always hide a bit of money for myself when I am in a relationship because you never know if you will be left or will need to leave. She taught it to me as fact, as generational knowledge and wisdom bestowed with love. But these are teachings that come from experiencing and witnessing all around what masculinity so often tries to do to female blackness.

Lemonade is also, understandably, a meditation on Black female anger – an emotion that Black women in the United States have been socialized to contain ever since the advent of the transatlantic slave trade. In 1981, Black, feminist, lesbian writer Audre Lorde told Black women that "anger expressed and translated into action in the service of our vision and our future is a liberating and strengthening act of clarification" (127). In *Lemonade*, Black female rage drips from sweet, sun-kissed smiles as Beyoncé saunters down a street in a frilly yellow dress and borrows a bat to smash cars, shop windows and fire hydrants on a hot day. Black female rage is clothed in designer wear, impossibly long cornrows and a large fur coat as Beyoncé flings an enormous engagement ring on the cement floor of an underground parking lot. *Lemonade* also turns Black female rage on the historical object of the lynching tree of the South in the United States where dismembered and charred Black people hung as white men and children posed for pictures. In 1939, Billie Holiday contained her rage-filled voice to paint a visceral, haunting picture of lynching in her song "Strange Fruit." In *Lemonade*, Black girls, Black women and Black mothers are dressed in period clothing and sit in the branches of the trees from which Black people – the "strange fruit" of the song's title – once hung. In *Lemonade*, generations of Black females stand beneath the trees' boughs and alongside the mothers of Black men slain by civilians and police officers.

In 1964, Nina Simone channelled her Black female rage in the singing of the song "Mississippi Goddamn" in commemoration of both the 16th Street Baptist Church bombing that killed four Black girls and the assassination of Black activist Medgar Evers by a white supremacist. In *Lemonade*, Beyoncé stands on a small wooden outdoor stage and performs a song about the illusiveness and pursuit of freedom for a small gathering of Black girls, Black women and Black mothers – some of whose children were killed by police officers and civilians. All throughout *Lemonade*, Black girls, Black women and Black mothers level their calm gaze directly at the camera. Their gaze is a silent, unwavering and unflinching one that stares down past and present. Their gaze connects the historical practice of lynching to the present-day practices of the school-to-prison pipeline, industrial prison complex and police violence against Black people.

Lemonade is an experimental work of popular art not only in content, but also in form. *Lemonade*, the project, successfully reimagines the genre of popular music in a way that no other artists of Beyoncé's era have done. It is an HBO special, a film and a music album supported by a tour named after "Formation." We were introduced to Beyoncé's new form of the visual album in 2013 when she released *Beyoncé*, her first visual album and fifth solo album. In the accompanying videos that document the album's impetus and creation, she declares "I see music. It's more than just what I hear" (" 'Self-Titled': Part 1" 00:04–00:10). Furthermore, she had long wanted, much to the dismay of record label executives, to shoot a video for each song so that her audience could experience the imagistic components of her music along with her. As discussed in Chapter 1, her first visual album garnered criticism because it was the first time that Beyoncé explicitly aligned herself with feminism, particularly in "★★★Flawless" featuring Nigerian author Chimamanda Ngozi Adichie. Black feminism worldwide has been profoundly influenced by the work of Black activists, artists and scholars in the United States. It speaks to the transnationalism of Black feminism in the digital era that the Black feminist material that Beyoncé quoted in her art came from Adichie, a Black feminist whose intellectual influences are anchored in Nigeria, which is a way away from the borders of the United States.

Reception of Beyoncé's pivot to Black feminist politics has been mixed. The most notable contention has come from leading Black feminist scholar bell hooks who, shortly after the release of Beyoncé's self-titled album in 2013, called Beyoncé "a terrorist [...] especially in terms of the impact on young girls" (hooks et al. 00:47:45–00:47:50). But is not that what much of popular culture does, especially to young people? Especially when pop culture demands from its audience the consumption of particular products, ideas and aesthetics? After the release of *Lemonade*, hooks asserted in an essay for *The Guardian* that the film "does not truly overshadow or change conventional sexist constructions of black female identity." The questions I am left with is when has that ever happened in popular culture and why would we expect the most influential pop artist to do anything that falls radically outside of the conventions of the genre of pop music? What do we make of our expectations of Beyoncé? What does freedom look like? Who is expected to draw near to a moral compass?

What is too often forgotten about Beyoncé is that she is a pop star working in an artistic genre that, like any other, has limitations. Beyoncé is, and has always been, a mainstream artist and there is little to nothing about her artistic history that suggests that she is interested in or even aware of the many intricate nuances of Black feminist theory. I read bell hooks' and others' expectations that Beyoncé push the cultural centre of pop music towards a radical Black feminist politic as symptomatic of larger frustrations with the mainstream. Misogyny, patriarchy, racism and white supremacy are bizarre, often terrifying, and resistant to change. In the face of these violent forms of oppression, many turn to Beyoncé with the expectation that she should use the platform that is her international cultural influence to lead overt social change. It is an unfair demand that I have made on numerous occasions in my research and teaching about Beyoncé. It is an unfair demand that I still make from time to time when she releases new work. It is an unfair demand for many reasons, not least of which is that anyone who has been on the inside of any industry, profession, organization or company knows how hard it is to make lasting institutional change. With the release in 2013 of *Beyoncé* (Self-Titled) and in 2016 of "Formation" and *Lemonade*, Beyoncé shifted the institution that is popular culture in the United States and beyond. We would be remiss if we forgot that popular culture is an institution that Beyoncé loves, that she has worked hard to dominate and that has rewarded her greatly. Effecting change in that context is a complex endeavour. It is also worth noting that critiques about a lack of social engagement and a radical Black politic were not part and parcel of other Black artists' careers, so why do we expect more from a female mega star than any other gender presentation?

Beyoncé, "Formation," *Lemonade* and The Formation World Tour that began in 2016 suggest, to me, that from about 2013 to 2016 Beyoncé turned her artistic attention to legacy. At that point in her career, she seemed to be no longer a pop artist motivated solely by the acquisition of fans, Grammy awards, chart placements, magazine covers, luxury goods, exclusive experiences and the like. In the song "6 Inch," she tellingly sings of a hard-working woman who seems to have at least two jobs and who saves her money instead of desiring or purchasing material items. For me this begs the question, what does this business mogul now understand the primary use of the accumulation of wealth to be for? Is it philanthropy, given her reference in "Formation" to being on track to amass the financial wealth of Bill Gates? And/or is she financially motivated to become the richest woman she can possibly be?

As I stood in my floor seats at The Formation World Tour concert, I noticed that the predominantly white women and the seemingly bored white men who accompanied them were not looking at Beyoncé perform on stage a mere nine rows away. Instead, they were either watching her image projected onto massive screens or watching her on the screen of their phones as they took pictures, recorded videos and posted to social media. Even when Beyoncé kneeled down and was mere inches from audience members, most of them still watched her through the screens of their phones as they recorded and took pictures. This made me realize that for them the experience of documenting her live performance (presumably as evidence to share on social media) was central to their experience of the live performance moment. It also means that Beyoncé, like other pop stars and other people, is now mediated through screens, which raises the question: what is the point of a live show at this moment? Beyoncé loves to perform. She said as much during the concert and it was abundantly clear by her impeccably produced, visually overwhelming and long performance that evening. Watching Beyoncé perform on tour is like watching a professional endurance athlete compete. For Beyoncé and other artists and entertainers who tour, the question is: how much longer will fans pay high ticket prices to physically attend live performances where they end up watching the show on big screens in the stadium or on personal devices? How much longer will they pay to attend shows with sometimes tens of thousands of other people when they could just watch on the screens of their choice somewhere else for less if not free? How Beyoncé and her peers continue to respond to these trends in popular culture will be fascinating to watch over the years.

But Beyoncé will respond. She always responds to shifts in popular culture. For decades Beyoncé has exhibited a rare characteristic for a pop star – consistency. She is always working, producing, recording, out on the town and making art that resonates with her fan base. That may be what I respect about Beyoncé the most: her ability to understand, mimic and direct culture and her ability to consistently make art and business moves regardless of her prior successes and failures – many of which are well documented, circulated and discussed online and in other venues. I was raised by a father who drilled into me what his mother taught him – dream big and work hard regardless of the outcome. Beyoncé has long exemplified an extraordinary work ethic.

My dad died when I was 22. We were close. We talked race, ethnicity, class, sexuality and feminism often. His influence on me has been and continues to be deep. When I was a child and a teen, he would often correct the cadence of my speech and my grammar. He challenged my ideas, expanded my thinking, encouraged me to think spiritually and philosophically. I miss him. I sang his favourite church hymn as breath left his body. His death was my undoing. I unravelled for about 19 months until I was completely undone and because life is relentless I was undone and yet still here. I was still here. There is something about the relentlessness of presence and of life's insistence on itself that has struck me as rude and magical ever since his death. I remember leaving the hospital, going outside and being vaguely surprised that cars were still driving on the streets, people were still walking, the sky was where it always is… My world has stopped, paused, come to a halt and yet life and the world offered no acknowledgement of my pain, my supreme disorientation, my loss. I was still here and to my surprise I was still moving. I learned during the months of my undoing that there are many ways to be here – there are states of consciousness, coherence and participation in the world that had prior to been unknown to me. It was not until I came undone that I realized that moving, talking, doing beyond the most basic bodily functions are choices and sometimes they are a series of choices that are difficult to make.

I unravelled and began to piece together a familiar and new self in the spring of 2001. It was during that time that Beyoncé's girl group Destiny's Child released the song "Survivor." Of course, I knew their most popular hits, but I had never followed them closely. I was vaguely aware of the news of their changing band members and possible dismantling, but I had not followed that saga closely either. But the song "Survivor" from the studio album of the same title hit the airwaves and my heart. I was 23 years old and in the process of rebuilding my life. Trying to get back on track, trying to piece myself together again and here were these young Black women singing about being survivors. Of course, we were surviving very different things, but the idea in the lyrics of reaching a point where one is unsure how to proceed while knowing that you will find a way made so much sense to me. "Survivor's" lyrics about self-doubt, external pressures and resilience perfectly expressed core themes in my life in my early 20s. I bought that Destiny Child's album, played the song on repeat and sung the chorus to myself for affirmation and motivation. Beyoncé's pop culture offering moved into my life and that hook, those beats and those lyrics became one of my go-to resources after my father's death.

I remember reading or seeing somewhere that Beyoncé had had the idea for the song and had penned the lyrics. I remember being impressed by her facing a difficult thing in her life head-on and making it into something popular that others could see themselves in. It was my first indication that Beyoncé was more than what I thought of as an average pop star and I have never been a pop music junkie. Not even that much of a pop culture fan really. I grew up in the 80s and listened to my fair share of Michael Jackson, Janet Jackson, Prince, The Pointer Sisters, Culture Club and Madonna, but by the 90s I was deep into dancehall reggae, conscious rap and neo-soul. I listened to artists like Buju Banton, Sizzla Kilanji, Tanya Stephens, Common Sense, Arrested Development, The Roots, Erykah Badu, and Meshell Ndegeocello. I knew pop music, but it was definitely not the soundtrack of my life. "Survivor" caught and kept my attention at the time because its chorus was an anthem that I could repeat to myself as I tried to move forward with conviction and hope. But beyond the resonant subject matter of the song I was also moved by its penmanship, by the fact that these were not asinine, coy, pop song lyrics fed to a girls group with pretty faces, decent voices and choreography. These were not lyrics that artists were being told to sing even though they did not like the song. No, "Survivor's" lyrics were penned by Beyoncé, a Black woman attempting to resolve and face a difficult situation and that resonated deeply with me as I tried to sort out my life.

About ten years later, I was invited by my employer, the University of Waterloo, to give a TEDx Talk on any subject of my choosing. I knew then that there was only one thing I needed to do even though it terrified me to my core. I had threaded my life together again and was making something meaningful out of it, but I was still heavy with internal monologues of shame and self-doubt. If I could stand in public and articulate the circumstances of my father's death and my own subsequent unravelling, then I hoped I could be freed from them. I wonder if there is any of that kind of impulse in Beyoncé's *Lemonade*. Her decision to suggest so much personal information is quite something and at the very least worthy of contemplation. The artist, feminist, queer person in me always chalks it back to that – a quest for a kind of freedom and the belief that truth-telling in some way will lead the way to that freedom even if the truth-telling will be critiqued by family, friends and society.

I think that this is an appropriate moment to pause and give a round of applause, a tip of the hat and a deep head nod of appreciation for Beyoncé. I think it is appropriate to pause and recognize the depth of her courage and internal conviction as a Black female artist working in popular culture in general and the music industry in particular. With *Lemonade*, Beyoncé exposed herself to public ridicule – all of the stereotypical words people throw at others, especially women and women-identified people, who dare remain in relationships that have been rife with infidelity and other lies. Except, in Beyoncé's case, she played out the inner workings of her personal relationship on an international stage which suggests, to me, that her commitment to herself and her expression of her life through music is greater than her fear of judgment. She did it with "Survivor" and again years later with *Lemonade* where she seemingly looked her marriage square in the eye. In an article for *Elle Magazine* in 2016, Melissa Harris-Perry reflects on the film and its complex visuals. She was initially most struck by *Lemonade*'s overt reference to suicide, which occurs from 4:03–4:29 when Beyoncé jumps from the roof of a high rise building and plunges stories down towards the cement sidewalk of a four-lane road. Harris-Perry describes Beyoncé's jump as "a terrifying answer to a question I have asked myself with frightening regularity in recent months. What if I just gave into the darkness I feel by going over the balcony?" At the moment of Beyoncé's impact on the ground, the cement gives way to deep waters in which Beyoncé ends up submerged without an oxygen tank. She swims against the backdrop of an opulent domestic life and though the swimming without oxygen suggests eventual drowning it also gestures towards a kind of acceptance because she is never seen flailing underwater.

What remains perhaps most compelling to me about *Lemonade* is Beyoncé's decision to steep it in African-American imagery, language and aesthetics. *Lemonade* was for Black women. While everyone else was invited to witness and observe, we were not all the intended primary audience. That is powerful and has impacted me professionally. What folks who critique Beyoncé, myself included at times, often forget is that she is working within the confines of popular culture. I cannot say it often enough. She is an artist with an art form that she is exploring, manipulating and mastering. Her medium is popular culture, and she is a disciplined practitioner of the genre. Asking, expecting, critiquing Beyoncé for not taking up the aesthetics of political art, feminist art, performance art etc. is unfair and understandable.

The terrain is complex. Popular culture evolves quickly. In 2013, Beyoncé received a backlash for calling women bitches in "Bow Down / I Been On" and "★★★Flawless"; in 2016 she said her financial wealth could one day match that of Bill Gates in "Formation"; and by 2017 Cardi B's explicit song "Bodak Yellow" about making money was the crossover hit that brought her into the mainstream.

"Bodak Yellow" is a rap song and video performance that flamboyantly describes how the attainment of economic means has elevated the social status and cultural capital of its female protagonist of colour, Cardi B, from that of other women. In particular, "Bodak Yellow" depicts, through its lyrics and accompanying video, how a woman can effectively manipulate patriarchal, classist structures to effectively pursue and attain a degree of financial success and social stature that can then be translated into wielding social, economic and sexual power over other people. This is the song that Cardi B rode to mainstream prominence as number one on the US Billboard Hot 100 chart in 2017. "Bodak Yellow" held that position for three consecutive weeks, which made Cardi B the second female rapper, after Lauryn Hill, to have a number one song as a solo performer.

I listened to "Bodak Yellow" and watched the video a few times in the months following its release. I bopped my head, recommended my spouse add it to a playlist he was making for a party and moved on. Two autumns later, I was listening to that same playlist on my driving commute to my job at the University of Waterloo. I was tired that morning but not from a fatigue that could be cured by sleep. I was tired because I was deep in thought doing something I had done countless times before over decades. I was contemplating how best to manage the latest iteration of institutionalized anti-Black racism and sexism that I had experienced as a Black, queer woman. In this particular instance, I was dealing with how these forms of discrimination recently manifested themselves again in my work as a professor and scholar in Canada and then "Bodak Yellow" began to play. I bopped my head as usual, but at some point I began to actually pay attention to the story being told. In that moment I experienced the lyrics to "Bodak Yellow" as a larger story about what it means to be a woman of colour who confronts others' vindictiveness, refuses to adhere to others' narrow definitions of her humanity and unabashedly celebrates the attainment of her goals. It made me feel like a superhero.

I was struck by Cardi B's imagistic, explicit, words and her visceral, relentless, delivery. I was moved by the freedom of expression that the combination of her words and delivery exhibited. It sounded like the freedom to not only discard people or disassociate herself from them but to also tell them in clear and succinct ways precisely why she refused to pay any attention to them and why they were irrelevant in her life. Her words were precise and unequivocal. They were powerful. I was inspired. I too wanted to reprimand the people in my profession who protect institutionalized white supremacy, patriarchy and heteronormativity. I too wanted to embarrass those in my profession who routinely espouse progressive rhetoric while firmly holding onto status quo practices and procedures that throw away the views and values of Black people, especially when we challenge whiteness, patriarchy, classism and heteronormativity. I too wanted to speak unfiltered to all those in my professional spheres whose comments and actions have sought to contain my \female blackness in order to exercise and affirm the power and privilege that their non-blackness, non-femaleness and/or non-queerness affords them.

Cardi B sounded free to me in "Bodak Yellow." The freedom and newness with which she expresses herself in that song is something that, at the time, felt unimaginable for me in my professional life. That day, I experienced "Bodak Yellow" as a song that aptly surmised and responded to the anti-Black racism and sexism that have shaped my professional life. For the three minutes and 43 seconds that is the song's duration, I was able to succinctly, cleverly and powerfully respond to the ways in which anti-Black racism and sexism are institutionalized in education systems without any consideration for the professional ramifications that invariably come when Black women's analysis centres the intersectionality that is Black womanhood. And I am reminded here of something that Amber J. Phillips said online, "Maintaining likeability is unrealistic for the Black woman" (@amberabundance).

Works Cited

Adichie, Chimamanda Ngozi. "We Should All Be Feminists: Chimamanda Ngozi Adichie at TEDxEuston." *TED Talks*, April 14, 2013, www.ted.com/talks/chimamanda_ngozi_adichie_we_should_all_be_feminists?language=en. Accessed September 4, 2022.
Beyoncé. *Lemonade*. Parkwood Entertainment, 2016.
———. "Daddy Lessons." *Lemonade*, Parkwood Entertainment, 2016.
———. *Beyoncé*. Parkwood Entertainment, 2013.
———. "Bow Down / I Been On." *Beyoncé*, produced by Tmbaland, Polow Da Don, Sonny Digital, Planet IV and Keyz, 2013. *SoundCloud*, July 21, 2014, https://soundcloud.com/beyonce/bow-down-i-been-on. Accessed August 29, 2022.
———. "★★★Flawless." *Beyoncé*, Columbia Records and Parkwood Entertainment, 2013.
———. "Daddy." *Dangerously in Love*, Sony Music Entertainment, 2003.
Cardi B. "Bodak Yellow." *Invasion of Privacy*, Atlantic Records, 2017.
Destiny's Child. "Survivor." Written by Anthony Dent, Beyoncé and Mathew Knowles. *Survivor*, Sony Music Entertainment, 2001.
DuBois, Shirley Graham. *I Gotta Home*. Alexander Street Press, 1942.

Harris-Perry, Melissa. "A Call and Response with Melissa Harris-Perry: The Pain and the Power of 'Lemonade.'" *Elle Magazine*, April 26, 2016, www.elle.com/culture/music/a35903/lemonade-call-and-response/. Accessed September 3, 2022.

Holiday, Billie. "Strange Fruit." Written by Lewis Allan. *Strange Fruit*, Atlantic Records, 1972

hooks, bell. "Beyoncé's Lemonade is capitalist money-making at its best." *The Guardian*, May 11, 2016, www.theguardian.com/music/2016/may/11/capitalism-of-beyonce-lemonade-album. Accessed September 2, 2022.

hooks, bell, et al. "bell hooks – Are you still a slave? Liberating the Black Female Body | Eugene Lang College." *YouTube*, uploaded by The New School, May 7, 2022, http://youtu.be/rJk0hNROvzs. Accessed September 2, 2022.

Keleta-Mae, Naila. "Black Girl Thought in the Work of Ntozake Shange." *Girlhood Studies: An Interdisciplinary Journal* vol. 12, no. 2, 2019, pp. 32–47.

Kennedy, Adrienne. *A Rat's Mass*. 1966. Alexander Street Press, 2008.

Lemonade. Directed by Beyoncé, Kahlil Joseph, Dikayl Rimmasch, Todd Tourso and Jonas Åkerlund. Parkwood Entertainment, 2016.

Lorde, Audre. *Sister Outsider: Essays and Speeches*. 1981. Crossing Press, 1984.

Phillips, Amber J. [@amberadundance]. Video of Phillips sharing her lessons for Black women. *Instagram*, November 29, 2018, www.instagram.com/p/Bqxmg6OF9wN/?hl=en. Accessed September 5, 2022.

"'Self-Titled': Part 1. The Visual Album." *YouTube*, uploaded by Beyoncé, December 13, 2013, http://youtu.be/IcN6Ke2V-rQ. Accessed September 4, 2022.

Shange, Ntozake. *Daddy Says*. Alexander Street Press, 2003.

Simone, Nina. "Mississippi Goddamn." *Nina Simone in Concert*, Phillips, 1964.

"US Billboard Hot 100 – week of October 7 2017." *Billboard*, October 7, 2017, www.billboard.com/charts/hot-100/2017-10-07/. Accessed October 12, 2022.

Wright, Nazera Sadiq. *Black Girlhood in the Nineteenth Century*. University of Illinois Press, 2016.

5 Longevity

Early in 2017 I read a tweet, which unfortunately I can no longer find, from Christina Sharpe that called for writers to write as though our readers are Black. Her words were revelatory. I am not sure exactly when it happened, but somewhere along the way I began to write for an audience that was not Black. There is a particular level of accountability that creating work primarily for a Black audience requires of the creator. Take, for example, the many thoughtful critiques from Black scholars, writers and public intellectuals who noted references to colourism in the lyrics and video of "Formation." There is also a depth of creativity that becomes available to Black writers when they are not bogged down by the time-consuming and creativity-draining labour required to explain concepts, ideas and realities to an audience because the audience already understands the artist's world as fact. For example, when Solange Knowles (Beyoncé's sister) sings the lyrics to "Don't Touch My Hair," Black audiences know that she is likely not talking to us. Black audiences know that we are the protagonist and the lyrics speak from our perspective in moments when we need to express the invasion of personal space that is someone touching our hair without permission.

One of my companions on my journey in Black feminism has been *Sister Outsider*, a small book of mighty essays and speeches by famed poet, scholar and activist Audre Lorde. Had I been fortunate enough to meet Audre Lorde in person, I probably would have wanted to call her Ms. Audre but would have called her Ms. Lorde instead. That is what I was raised to do by my Jamaican-born parents. There is something more intimate about Ms. Audre than Ms. Lorde. That first name shows knowledge of each other, a shared ground, a closeness and still respect. But, I would have called her Ms. Lorde upon meeting her in reverence of her age and vast experience. I am thinking here about naming as a small way of connecting with our feminist elders, feminist contemporaries and feminist friends. I am thinking about how it helps me structure memories and relationships. It is part of how I make, form

DOI: 10.4324/9780367808488-5

and sustain connections in environments that are hostile to blackness and seek to annihilate Black life.

That is what Sharpe's tweet about writing for Black people brought me back to. I think that for some Black women, that is precisely how other Black women's music, scholarship, poetry, videos, visual art and films make us feel. It is as though, in the brief moments of engaging with their work, we are able to move through the world with these women, share their feelings and be influenced by their perspectives. I think that for some Black women, when we engage with the art, scholarship and online presence of other Black women, it is not just as passive audience members with no stakes in the game. Our connections with Black women through these mediums are as meaningful to us as are our online and in-person catch-up sessions with our sister-friends. I think that this is also why some Black women want so much from and for our Black female artists. I tend to not only want them to share their artistic expression – I also want them to take on and change the systemic forces of oppression that attempt to erode and shorten Black life. I recognize that that is a tall order, especially when I know that accomplished Black female artists on these lands face the same racism, sexism and other forms of oppression with which so many of us are profoundly familiar.

Ultimately, what makes Beyoncé most compelling to me is that she is a Black woman with decades of experience steering the cultural zeitgeist from the United States of America, where Black people have endured horrific violence for centuries. Against this complex backdrop of racial politics in the United States, Beyoncé's decades of success signal longevity in a notoriously fickle and patriarchal industry. Beyoncé's company, Parkwood Entertainment, creates, produces and markets the stories she wants to tell and then disseminates them directly to an online audience bigger than the population of Canada. She combines her voice, appearance and public persona with an astute manipulation of audio and visual media to tell the stories that she wants to tell to the audiences that she wants to reach. That is a remarkable amount of power for a Black woman to have amassed in an industry predominantly run by men in a country with a history of chattel slavery. Beyoncé's influence on popular culture is immense as is the impact of her portrayals of female blackness that spill over into and shape our daily lives.

Works Cited

Beyoncé. "Formation." *Lemonade*. Parkwood Entertainment, 2016.
Lorde, Audre. *Sister Outsider: Essays and Speeches*. Crossing Press, 1984.
Sharpe, Christina [@hystericalblkns]. *Twitter*, 2017.
Solange. "Don't Touch My Hair." With performances by Sampha. *A Seat at the Table*, Columbia Records, September 30, 2016.

Index

Adichie, Chimamanda 11, 18, 32
Allred, Kevin 2
Arrested Development 35

Badu, Erykah 35
Banton, Buju 35
Beyoncé: as commercial brand 7; consistency of 34; control over her own career and identity 7; displays of body and wealth in performances of 1–2, 33–4; empowerment of young women by 10; as modern-day feminist 7–8, 32; as part of Destiny's Child 9, 13–14, 34–5; public persona of 7–8, 11, 15; as research subject 1–5, 41; sexualization of 16–17; use of social media by 8, 9–12
Beyoncé (Self-Titled) 4, 7–18, 32–3; "Bow Down/I Been On" 8–11, 14–15; critiques of 11–12; "Flawless" 12–15, 18
Black girlhood 5, 30
Black Joy Mixtape, The 27
Black Lives Matter movement 23, 25, 27
Black masculinity 29–30
Black Panther Party 23, 24
Black women 11; in academia 20, 26, 35–6, 40–1; addressed by "Bow Down/I Been On" 8–10; anger and socialization of 30–1; as feminists 8, 13, 23–4, 32, 40–1; "Formation" and 25–6; marriage and 29–30; sexualization of 17; violence against 31; Women's March, 2017, and 26–7

"Bodak Yellow" 37–8
"Bow Down/I Been On" 8–11, 14–15, 37

Cardi B 8, 37–8
Carter, Blue Ivy 8
Carter, Sean "Jay-Z" 8, 21, 29
Coldplay 23
Common Sense 35
Crissle 11, 12
Culture Club 35

"Daddy" 29–30
Daddy Says 30
Daly, Mary 25
Davis, Angela 24
Destiny's Child 9, 13–14, 34–5
Didion, Joan 15
"Don't Hurt Yourself" 29
"Don't Touch My Hair" 40
"Drunk in Love" 1, 2
Du Bois, Shirley Graham 30

Elle Magazine 36

feminism: of Beyoncé 7–8, 17; Black 8, 13, 23–4, 32, 40–1; sexualization of women and 16–17; Women's March, 2017, and 26–7
"Flawless" 12–15, 18, 37
"Formation" 20–1, 33; beat and lyrics of 21–2; Black feminism and 23–4; as complex meditation on female blackness 21–2; performed at Superbowl 50 halftime show 22–5;

reach and impact of 23; video of 21–2, 25
Fury, Kid 11

Gates, Bill 37
"Grown Woman" 16
Guardian, The 32
Gyn/Ecology 25

Hall, Stuart 17
Harris-Perry, Melissa 36
Hart, Erika 27
Hatton, Erin 17
Henderson, Mae Gwendolyn 22
Hit Boy 8–9
Holiday, Billie 24, 31
hooks, bell 11, 16, 32
Hurricane Katrina 22

I Gotta Home 30
Instagram 11–12
iTunes 12

Jackson, Janet 35
Jackson, Michael 35

Kennedy, Adrienne 30
Keyz 9
Kilanji, Sizzla 35
King, Martin Luther Jr. 22
Knowles, Mathew 29–30
Knowles, Solange 15, 40
Knowles, Tina 30

Lemonade 29–38; anger explored in 30–1; "Daddy Lessons" 29–30; "Don't Hurt Yourself" 29; marriage explored in 29–30; "Sorry" 29; truth-telling in 35–6; as visual album 29, 31–2
Lorde, Audre 11, 25, 31, 40–1

Madonna 35
Martin, Trayvon 23
Matsoukas, Melina 21
McMahon, Ed 13
Meeropol, Abel 24
Mike WiLL Made It 21
Minaj, Nicki 8, 15

Missing and Murdered Indigenous Women's marches 27
"Mississippi Goddamn" 31
Mya, Messy 22

Ndegeocello, Meshell 35
Noisey 20–1

Obama, Barack 15
Obama, Michelle 9

Phillips, Amber J. 27, 38
Planet IV 9
Pointer Sisters, The 35
Polow Da Don 9
Prince 35

Ramsey, Francesca Leigh 12
Rat's Mass, A 30
Read, The 11
Rihanna 8
Rolling Stone 17
Roots, The 35
Roy, Arundhati 27
"Run the World (Girls)" 10

Senofonte, Marni 21
sexualization of women 16–17
Shange, Ntozake 30
Sharpe, Christina 40–1
Simone, Nina 31
Sister Outsider 25, 40–1
Sonny Digital 9
"Sorry" 29
SoundCloud 10
Sremmurd, Rae 21
Star Search 13
Stephens, Tanya 35
"Strange Fruit" 4, 24, 31
"Surprise!" 12
"Survivor" 34–5

Tidal 23
Timbaland 9
Time Magazine 16–17
Trautner, Mary Nell 17
Trump, Donald 26
Truth, The 22

Tumblr 8, 9
Turini, Shiona 21

Walker, Jazmine 27
West, Beryl 30

Women's March, 2017 26–7
Wright, Nazera Sadique 30

Year of Magical Thinking, The 15
YouTube 11, 20, 23

For Product Safety Concerns and Information please contact our EU representative GPSR@taylorandfrancis.com
Taylor & Francis Verlag GmbH, Kaufingerstraße 24, 80331 München, Germany

www.ingramcontent.com/pod-product-compliance
Lightning Source LLC
Chambersburg PA
CBHW051800230426
43670CB00012B/2376